GCD BOOKS

Visit GCDiscipleship.com/Books

A Pastor's Guide for Everyday Mission: Navigating the Paradox of Leading God's People and Pursuing God's Mission by Ben Connelly

Multiply Together: A Guide to Sending and Coaching Missional Communities by Brad Watson

Small Town Mission: A Guide for Mission-Driven Communities by Aaron Morrow

Make, Mature, Multiply: Becoming Fully-Formed Disciples of Jesus by Brandon D. Smith

Follow us on Twitter @GCDiscipleship

RENEW

HOW THE GOSPEL MAKES US NEW

JIM HUDSON

ISBN-13: 978-0692853337 (GCD Books)
ISBN-10: 0692853332

Cover design by Mathew B. Sims
MathewBryanSims.com

TABLE OF CONTENTS

INTRODUCTION
HOW THE GOSPEL
MAKES US NEW

So how exactly do we grow spiritually? Is it simply a case of willpower and conquering our sin through perseverance and effort? In many parts of Christianity that is exactly what is believed. Growth is simply equated with obedience. We read the Bible and go to church to understand how we are supposed to live rightly and then our job as Christians is to try and do just that. God's grace is rarely mentioned here.

In other parts of the Christian church, the therapeutic model is what is taught as the model for change/growth. Under the therapeutic model we try to understand how our wounds and dysfunctional family systems hinder our God views and contribute to our own dysfunctional behavior (which is rarely called sin). Our role is to apply wisdom principles (usually a blend of man-centered approaches and biblical proof texts) to enable us to overcome our problems. God's grace is hard to find here too.

Still other approaches call into question the very idea of spiritual growth, seeing growth as something that may or may not even happen. This is the "let go, let God" approach. The focus here is on God's unconditional approval of us as we are, without regard to whether we ever change. This approach may mention the grace of God, but it is a very anemic grace that lacks any power. Instead, it is a false grace that can often lead to permissiveness.

Each of these approaches has some parts that are true. God's word does indeed give us a template for living, and throughout Scripture there are exhortations for us to engage in personal effort to live rightly. And it is also true that the wounds we receive from the sins of others affect us and can shape our own sin tendencies. And it is also true that, in Christ (an important caveat), we are loved by God apart from our growth as a Christian.

Yet all of the above approaches to growth are incomplete and, at some level, plain wrong. If we have the ability to overcome sin through our own effort, then Jesus died for no reason. And our wounds are not our greatest problem—it's our own sin. No wisdom of man can overcome that problem. And God clearly cares about our growth. In fact, Romans 8:29 says that he has predestined us to be conformed to the image of his son. It would be unloving of God to not care about our daily fight against sin because it causes so much suffering in us. Because God loves us, he wants us to grow and to experience victory in our fight against sin. In fact, the Bible says he wants us to be dead to sin (Rom. 6:11).

This study is aimed at showing how the gospel, the means by which God initially brings us to salvation, is also the means by which God continues to save us for our ongoing growth, which the bible calls "sanctification." Because of our faith in the completed and perfect work of Jesus Christ (through his life, death and resurrection), the power of God (grace) has been made available to us to fight against sin, to grow into the image of Christ and in so doing to glorify God. My hope for you is that through this study you will see how much God loves you and all that he has done for you in Christ. That will in turn cause you to love him more and love your sin less. Love God and hate sin. That is how we grow.

How This Book Is Laid Out

The book consists of twelve lessons. The lessons generally build on one another, so it is important to work through all the material in the order it is laid out. Each lesson includes Scripture that should be studied, a devotional that unpacks the biblical material and concepts, and discussion questions that help you integrate the material into your own life and serve as the content for small group discussions. I want to stress the importance of actually writing out the answer to your questions. This will help you think more deeply about the material, which will help move it from your head down to your heart.

Toward the back of the study there is also a section called "Renew Journal." This section serves as a project component where you will take material from certain lessons and do a more in-depth personal study. For example, in Lesson 5 we will discuss heart idols that relate to comfort, control and people. In the Renew Journal you will be encouraged to examine certain areas of your life to see if these heart idols are present. Remember, this study is meant to be a tool for you to apply the gospel to your life, so I strongly encourage you not to skip these exercises that will show you where the gospel is actually needed. The lesson will clearly indicate whether a project is included in the Renew Journal for that particular lesson. (About half of the lessons include a project.) The work you do on your projects will typically not be shared during the group time.

Most importantly, while you will read Scripture, answer your questions, and complete your projects individually, this study is not designed to be done alone. We need the counsel of other believers in order to be encouraged, celebrated, prayed for and sometimes even admonished. That is the beauty of being a part of the family of God. So I encourage you to do this study in a small group and also to meet outside of the group time to share material that may not be covered in the group (like the project material).

Be Encouraged

Finally, some of you may be going through this study because you find yourself in the middle of a crisis. It may be a crisis that your own sin caused or it may have been caused by someone else's sin. Regardless, you may be struggling with how this gospel you keep hearing about is of any practical help to you. I want you to know that I have been there at points in my own life, wrestling with my own addictions and idols. Please know that I wrote this study especially for you because regardless of what others may tell you, the gospel is your only hope . . . and is in fact a very real hope. This gospel of Jesus Christ is the very power of God (Rom. 1:16), the same power that raised Jesus' lifeless body from the grave and which has been made available to us who believe (Eph. 1:19-20). I can tell you, it is the only hope for me.

I hope you find the study helpful and most importantly find God to be gracious and glorious.

May His Grace and Peace Be With You Always,

JIM HUDSON

LESSON 1
THE STORMS WE FACE

Read Scripture:

- Genesis 1-3 (Read this passage in one setting as you would a story.)
- Romans 8:20-22

Contemplate It:

On May 3, 1999 the City of Moore, Oklahoma was leveled by a monster F5 tornado. It's winds were clocked at over 300 mph, the highest wind speed ever recorded on earth. It lasted for over 85 minutes, traveled 38 miles, and was at times a mile wide. The damage was shocking. Thirty-six people died and over $1 billion in property was destroyed. Incredibly, over the next 14 years Moore would be hit by three more monster tornadoes—two F4's in 2003 and 2010 and another F5 in 2013.

Disasters like tornadoes, earthquakes, and hurricanes terrify us because they remind us how truly powerless we are. You can't warn a tornado away. You can't try to avoid an earthquake. Kind words won't calm down the winds of a hurricane. While modern science has given us a better understanding of the causes of disasters, that understanding does little to give us power over them. The world is deadly, and at times it seems like it is trying to kill us.

But things were not always this way . . . the world was once safe for us. In Genesis 1 and 2 we see a "good" world that had been created by God to display his glory. There was nothing lacking in it. And in the world God made he also created a garden, a template for what he wanted his whole world to become. In that garden he placed a man and a woman—Adam and Eve—to keep it and to extend it to all the wildness of the earth. And everything worked as it was supposed to in this new world. Everything had *shalom*, a Hebrew word that means "peace." Shalom was in gravity, the weather, the DNA of living things—in everything, including in Adam and Eve. All was exactly as it should be, everything working together to glorify God. Adam and Eve did not live in fear of F5 tornadoes or earthquakes. They did not fear one another. You and I have never seen that garden full of shalom, but we were made for it. Our hearts ache for it. Every day.

But in Genesis 3, the enemy of God, Satan, tempted the man and woman to doubt God's goodness and to prize a created thing (fruit!) above God himself. The sin under Adam's and Eve's sin was pride, a belief that their ways and their thoughts were better than God's. The man and woman rebelled against God and when they did, shalom was lost everywhere . . . it was lost from the weather, in our DNA and in our hearts. Nothing worked right anymore. Creation became hopelessly corrupted and futile (Rom. 8:20-22.) The world became deadly. We became deadly.

The immediate cause of the 1999 Moore tornado was a phenomenon meteorologists call a supercell thunderstorm, which formed along a line of dry air from the western U.S. colliding with humid air over the central plains. But the corruption of creation brought about by the Fall in Genesis 3 is what really caused the 1999 tornado in Moore. Because of our sin, nothing works right anymore. The corrupting influence of sin causes all sorts of storms in our lives—whether it is sickness, broken marriages, pornography, drug and alcohol abuse, and everything else. Whatever is causing your pain or causing you to inflict pain on others is, at its root, caused by the Fall of man in Genesis 3. The power source of your sin is the same power that pushes tornadoes through subdivisions and tsunamis over islands.

And if this is true (and God's Word says it is true), then we are fools if we think that we can solve our brokenness and corruption on our own. Sin is an F5 tornado bearing down on us and we have no way to stop it or possibility to escape it ourselves. Our hope must come from someplace (or really, *someone*) other than ourselves.

Discuss It:

1. In what ways are you (apart from God working in you) just as powerless over the sin that is in you as the weather that is around you? Be specific.

2. In what ways do you tend to describe your struggles as something other than sin? For example, by calling your sin a bad choice, mistake, someone else's fault, etc.

3. Discuss the ways in the past you have tried on your own to change. Did it work? Why or why not?

4. What is the F5 tornado in your life right now? Do you *really* believe it is too big for you to overcome on your own?

Summarize It:

In your own words (based on Scripture) summarize how the struggles you face every day are ultimately caused by the Fall and sin.

Apply It:

Record in the Renew Journal some of the destruction caused by your sin.

LESSON 2
THE HELP WE NEED

Read Scripture:
- Ezekiel 36:25-27
- 2 Corinthians 5:17-21
- Ephesians 1-2:10

Contemplate It:

The boom shook our whole house. My first thought was that the hot water heater exploded, so I ran downstairs to check it out. Nothing wrong there. I then ran outside to see if something had hit the house. Nothing. Then, for some reason, I decided that it had to be an earthquake. I have no idea why. I just decided that. Convinced that I was right, I went to the USGS web site expecting to see reports of a big earthquake hitting Arkansas. No reports yet, but I was sure they would start coming in.

Then my wife popped my bubble and told me it was definitely not an earthquake. Since she was living in San Francisco in 1989 when the last big earthquake hit, she actually knew something about the subject. I had never been in an earthquake, and, as it turned out, I still had not been. The boom we heard was actually caused by the spring attached to the garage door breaking.

Had I remained convinced of my mega-earthquake theory, then perhaps I might have asked a builder to come by and check our house for damage. Since the problem turned out to be the garage door, I called the garage door company. It works the same way with our personal struggles. How we diagnose a problem determines where we go to find help for the problem. If I believe my problem is you, then I will invest a lot of time and emotional energy trying to convince you to change. If, on the other hand, I see the problem originating with me, but refuse to see it as sin, then the help I look for will likely reflect the self-help approach offered by our culture.

Sadly, the self-help approach to change is the most popular approach for professing Christians. It often validates our beliefs that we can change if we just talk to the right person, read the right book, get the right insight, apply the right technique, and maximize the right effort. At other times the self-help approach provides us an excuse for why we don't have to change (encouraging us to embrace our "wounds" as the underlying reason for our dysfunction). We like the self-help approach because it leaves us in the driver's seat. We keep the *illusion* of control.

But as we discussed in the previous lesson, the fundamental problem that we face in life is that we are sinful people, living amongst other sinful people, in a broken world. And if we believe that the fundamental problem we face in life is how to overcome sin then we also have to face the truth that we cannot overcome it through our own effort. We are part of the problem, not the solution to the problem. We cannot stare down that F5 sin tornado barreling toward us. The prophet Jeremiah recognized that this sin problem was found in our hearts more than our brains. Jeremiah said our hearts are so bad that they are beyond our own understanding (Jer. 17:9). If we want to deal with our sin, we have to deal with our hearts first. And *we* can't change our hearts. But God can.

Immediately after the Fall, as God pronounced curses on Adam, Eve and the rest of creation, he also made a promise. In Genesis 3:15, he said that the offspring of the woman would someday bruise the head of the serpent. This is the first hint of the gospel, that God would send a redeemer to defeat the serpent and undo the effects of the Fall. Rather than simply snapping his fingers to make everything right again, God began to patiently unfold a plan of redemption centered on his son, Jesus Christ. Ezekiel prophesied that through Jesus God would exchange hearts made of stone for hearts made of flesh (Ez. 36:26). A stone heart symbolizes the hardness that sin causes. And things made of stone are definitely not alive. How would God bring about our redemption? By putting his Spirit within us, he makes us alive (a "heart of flesh" symbolizes life) and gives us the power to think and act differently (v. 27).

But none of this is true for you or me apart from our personal, trusting faith in the gospel. It is one thing to believe intellectually that a rope can hold your weight. It is faith to tie that rope around your waist and repel off a cliff. Too many of us have a religious, informational understanding of the gospel, but lack real faith in it. We may think we have enough faith to be saved from hell, but doubt God's power to fight against sin in this life. But here is the terrifying truth: That type of faith has *no power at all*. It cannot help us in this life, and it will not save us from hell after this life.

So what exactly is the "gospel?" Read 2 Corinthians 5:21, which is a great summary of the gospel:

> *For our sake he [God] made him to be sin who knew no sin [Christ], so that in him we might become the righteousness of God.*

There is a lot about the gospel packed into this short verse. First, God takes the initiative on our behalf to save us; he acts "for our sake." God is the one who graciously saves us, without us earning it in any way. How does he save us? Through the atoning death of Christ on the cross. (Atonement is a term you may hear from time to time. It simply means that Jesus died in your place to satisfy God's just demands that your sin be punished.) God places our sin on a sinless Christ, and gives us the righteousness of Christ in return. That righteousness of Christ comes about because we are now "in Christ," which is just a theological way of saying that the Holy Spirit now lives in us, joining us to Christ and applying all of the benefits of the gospel to us. If you have faith in this wonderful gospel, then the Apostle Peter says that everything you need for life and Godliness has now been given to you (2 Pt. 1:3). God's grace, the very power of God himself, is now available to you.

So, as you face the sin tornado in your own life, where does your help come from? From yourself? Someone else? Or from Jesus Christ? Do you have faith in a gospel that is powerful enough to defeat your sin?

Discuss It:

1. Draw a picture of yourself as you think God sees you. (You will not have to share your artwork in the small group, so don't panic.) How would you describe how God sees you? (Be honest.) Do you think how he sees you changes when you sin?

2. Describe your belief in the gospel. Is it just information you understand about God or is it a hope you believe in that helps you right here, right now? If you doubt or do not believe in the gospel at all, please feel the freedom to share that, but also be willing to consider the hope that the gospel provides.

3. 2 Corinthians 5:18 states that because of the gospel of Jesus Christ we are now "reconciled" to God. Why do you think that is important?

4. Write out all the spiritual blessings you see in Ephesians 1 that we have through faith in Jesus Christ (adoption, inheritance, redemption, forgiveness, etc.). Which blessing is the biggest encouragement to you today? Why? How does that blessing help you to fight against your sin struggle?

5. Ephesians 1:19-20 makes a bold, crazy-sounding promise. The Apostle Paul says the same power of God that brought Jesus back from the dead is available to us who have faith in Jesus Christ. That means supernatural power (as opposed to human effort/willpower) is available to you to fight against porn, anger, drugs, anxiety, eating disorders, unforgiveness, control, etc. Do you regularly experience this power in your life as you fight against sin? Why or why not?

Summarize It:

In your own words (based on Scripture) summarize how the gospel of Jesus Christ is the help you must look to in order to change.

Apply It:

Record in the Renew Journal some of your struggles with believing that the gospel is the help you really need to fight against your sin struggles.

LESSON 3
WATER FOR DRY SOULS

Read Scripture:
- Jeremiah 17:7-8
- Romans 6:1-14; 7:14-25
- Galatians 5:16-24

Contemplate It:

My wife Leigh and I are blessed with a home that we truly love. Some of the features of the house that we enjoy most are the great outdoor living spaces. We love sitting outside, taking in the beauty of what God has made. But there is one part of our outdoor space that is not particularly attractive. It's a 2-3 yard wide strip between our driveway and our neighbor's lot that is mainly full of weeds. If our entire yard looked that way I doubt if we would have ever purchased the house.

On one side of the driveway we have thick, green grass, flowers and shrubs. On the other side of the driveway, we have little grass, but lots of weeds, rocks and dirt. So, why the difference? It's simple—irrigation. On the "pretty" side we have a sprinkler system that waters the grass and flowerbeds during Arkansas's hot, dry summers. On the "ugly" side of our house there are no sprinkler heads so it never gets water (unless it rains). If you look closely at the ugly side you can see zoysia that has been there since the whole yard was first sodded over a decade ago. But without irrigation, over time, weeds have overtaken the grass and choked it out. And without water, the exact same thing would happen to the pretty side too.

Christians are like my yard. They have two sides. One part of us is controlled by our spirit, which is similar to the

23

pretty, green part of my yard. If you are a Christian, your spirit has been sealed and is being safeguarded by the Holy Spirit. This part of you is "new" because it has already experienced a resurrection. Sin has been forever expelled from that part of you. It remains free of weeds because of the irrigating power of the Holy Spirit. This part of us bears fruit (joy, peace, self-control, etc.) in keeping with our salvation. It is the part that lives in the truth declared by Scripture, that we are dead to sin and are now walking in newness of life (Rom. 6:4). Walking in newness of life means your spirit shapes your thoughts to focus on the beauty of who Christ is *for you* and seeks to control your bodily behaviors so that the actions you take are for the glory of God (Col. 3:17).

The other part of us is what the Bible calls "flesh." The flesh is like the weeds that are in control of the un-irrigated side of my driveway. It is where sin still has *some* control over us, in what we think about and in our bodily behaviors. When the flesh is in control of us, we forget or deny the truths of Scripture and actually see sin as attractive. In fact, we see sin as something *we need*. When our flesh is in control we think about ourselves most and Christ least. Flesh bears a different type of fruit, the weeds of sin (such as anger, envy, idolatry, sexual immorality, etc).

Because we have a new spirit but old flesh, we are simultaneously saints and sinners. But our flesh can be controlled by our spirit. Since God himself lives in and controls our spirit, our flesh must submit to the desires of our spirit. To grow as a Christian means to grow in that part of you controlled by the spirit and for that part of you controlled by your flesh to shrink. But how?

Let's start first with what doesn't work. Most of the time we spend a lot of effort trying to restrain our flesh or trying to get it to do things it does not want to do. We typically do that with will power, which is never very effective over the long-term. Why? Because your self-will lives in your flesh, so that makes it part of the problem, not the solution. Here's an example. Let's say that you want to stop looking lustfully at the opposite sex. When we try that with will power ("bouncing our eyes" is what some books suggest) we might be successful for a while, but we have done nothing to change our desire to look. So, sooner or later we give in (and then typically go on some type of lust-spree looking at everything all the time).

Same thing happens with diets. We restrain our appetites using self-will, then give in, eat more and eventually gain more weight than we had before we began the diet. Behavior change based on self-will is like me spray-painting the ugly side of my yard green. The surface appearance has changed (for awhile) but I'll still get weeds because nothing has been done to address the fundamental problem that caused the weeds. That is all flesh-driven strategies will ever do, make cosmetic changes without addressing the root cause of sin. And the root cause of sin is the Holy Spirit not controlling us, which results in our minds and bodies not worshipping Christ and living in submission to his reign over our lives.

Trying to get our flesh to behave properly is what drives legalistic, religious approaches to change. It is basically the "try harder" strategy that exhausts us spiritually, emotionally and physically. It ruins our souls. It is also why so many Christians mistakenly believe that their faith is of no practical help to them in growing/changing. But remember, Jesus came and died for our sins because we simply cannot change ourselves. If we could, *then Jesus died for no reason.*

The only hope we have to fight against our sin is the grace of Jesus Christ. As we discussed in the last lesson, through faith in Jesus Christ we receive his saving, transforming grace. This is the very same power that God used to bring Jesus Christ back from the dead (Eph. 1:19-20), so sin doesn't stand a chance against grace. The Apostle Paul tells us that wherever there is sin, grace increases more and more (Rom. 5:20). That means we will never run out of grace, which is good news!

So how does this grace thing work, practically? We have to begin with faith. Many never experience the transforming grace of Jesus Christ because they doubt that it is of any benefit to them. They think salvation is incomplete, believing that God may save us from hell, but he does not offer any meaningful help right now. How sad . . . and untrue. But the Bible says something different. Instead, the Bible promises an all-sufficient grace, right here, right now:

"And God is able to make all grace abound to you, so that having all sufficiency in all things at all times, you may abound in every good work." – 2 Corinthians 9:8

The "good work" God has called all of us to is to put off our sin and to grow in righteousness. Author and psychologist Heath Lambert describes the way we receive God's transforming grace this way:

"Transforming grace works when you believe that Jesus gives it to you. The moment you believe in Jesus' grace to change you, you are changing. The more you continue to believe it, the more you will continue to change."

Faith leads to grace, and grace fills up your spirit so that it (not your flesh) fights against sin. That's the point of Galatians 5:16, we walk by the Spirit, so that we don't give in to the flesh. Grace makes you aware of the Spirit of Christ living inside of you who has already defeated sin. Grace reminds you that those sinful thoughts you have are just silly compared to the incredible spiritual blessings you have in Christ. Grace begins to create in you a desire to act differently, to want to be like Christ, not because you "ought to" but because you want to use your body as a way to worship Christ (Rom. 12:1). Grace is God's love invading more and more of your life, like a ripple from a rock thrown into a pond.

So growing as a Christian means that we must keep growing in grace (2 Pt. 3:18). Our role is to engage in effort that makes us aware of the present availability of God's grace. This effort includes things like reading our Bibles, prayer, worship, confession, community, and many other activities we will talk about in coming lessons. These activities ARE NOT ways to impress God or some religious obligation we have. Instead, these efforts, which we call "means of grace," are nothing more than turning on the sprinkler system so that grace can irrigate our dry souls. They remind us of all that Christ has done for us and all that he has given to us. That increases our love for Christ, diminishes our love for sin, which then increases our faith, provides us even more grace, and fills our spirit even more.

And with the water of grace splashing on our spirits, we will then be like the pretty side of my yard, full of life and bearing good fruit. Furthermore, that healthy, "green" part of us will begin to invade those parts of us controlled by the flesh, full of the weeds of sin. As Jeremiah says, we will then become "like a tree planted by water, that sends out its roots by the stream and does not fear when heat comes, for its leaves remain green" (Jer. 17:8).

For many of us, this is a new way of thinking about change. We have spent years "trying harder" to be better. But remember, trying harder is a failed strategy that just leads to shame and more sin. Stop trying. Start believing. Trust that when you are weak, God is so strong. And turn on the waters of grace!

Discuss It:

1. Quite often our sin struggles follow predictable patterns, or cycles, where our core beliefs and shame leave us open to temptation, leading to sin, which then reinforces our beliefs and shame. It turns into an ever-deepening spiral. In what ways do you see sin patterns or cycles at work in your life?

2. Share some ways you have tried to use will power to change. How did you feel when you failed?

3. In your own words, what does it mean to walk by the Spirit (Gal. 5:16). How does this help in your struggle against your sin?

4. Have you ever had a season when you felt you were walking by the Spirit (not by the flesh/will-power) and experiencing victory over sin? Describe what that was like.

5. How often do you use God's means of grace like Scripture reading, prayer, confession, etc.? How have these been a help to you in your fight against sin?

Summarize It:

In your own words (based on Scripture) summarize the difference between trying to change based on your self-will rather than being changed by the grace of Jesus Christ.

Apply It:

Record in the Renew Journal some of your patterns of sin struggles.

LESSON 4
OUR WRECKAGE

Read Scripture:
- Hebrews 12:1-2
- 2 Corinthians 13:5-9
- Colossians 3:5-15
- 1 John 1:7-10
- Romans 8:31-39

Contemplate It:

Most of us remember well the events of September 11, 2001. Our memories are sharp because we watched it on television as it happened. After the twin 110-story towers fell they collapsed several other buildings in the World Trade Center complex. What remained was a massive debris pile of twisted steel and concrete. In the weeks that followed the initial rescue efforts, the work shifted to recovery and debris removal. But the crews needed more information about how the debris was distributed at Ground Zero so it could be removed safely. There were voids several stories deep over basements, parking garages and subway lines that could easily collapse under the weight of construction equipment. So NASA stepped in to help. It flew a jet with special radar over Ground Zero to map the debris field. The map NASA produced helped the workers safely remove the 1.8 million tons of debris over the next several months.

You and I have our own debris field. We walk around in it every day. It's the debris of sin and all the consequences and pain that it creates for us, our family and friends. We know our sin is there but we spend a lot of energy trying not to look at it. We feel shame about our sin and the prospect of facing it overwhelms us. Sure, we may acknowledge that we are sinners, but we keep that acknowledgment pretty general, never really owning the specific things about us that need to change. And that type of thinking just keeps us stuck. The author of Hebrews likens sin to a weight that slows us down in our race to maturity as a Christian (Heb. 12:1). And the sin that we habitually go back to again and again sticks so close it trips us up. We will never be able to lay these sins aside unless we can first admit they are there. And we can't admit something unless we can see it. So we need a map of our own sin debris field so we can face our sin.

In order to map our sin we engage in the spiritual practice of self-examination (2 Cor. 13:5). This is a means of grace that God uses to grow us into the image of Christ. How does self-examination work? First, we pray for the grace of Christ to shine like a flashlight into our lives and illuminate what is there. And then we just become willing to see ourselves as we truly are. Honestly. Without needing to defend, explain or minimize, we look at our sin. And we are not surprised when we find it. In fact, it is the willingness to see our sin that shows God's truth is actually in us (1 Jn. 1:8). And once we see our sin clearly, we can then ask God to haul it off, or as the Bible puts it, we can seek God's grace to put that sin off so we can put on Christlikeness (Col. 3:5-15).

In order to help us to become aware of the sorts of sins we typically struggle with, we'll spend the next three lessons discussing specific types of sins that are common to us (after all, there is nothing new under the sun). We'll look at sins involving comfort (like substance abuse, gluttony, porn, greed), control (like anger, eating disorders, fear, pride), and people (like approval-seeking, relationship addiction, adultery). We will also focus on shame and bitterness. And after we map out these sins we'll know exactly what sins we need to repent of and where God's transforming grace is needed most in our lives. The discussion questions will help you understand the principles better, but it is critical that you spend time in your Renew Journal where you will actually practice self-examination.

Here's one word of caution as we begin this task together. We have an enemy who loves to accuse us. So expect that as you look honestly at yourself, Satan will seek to heap shame on you for your sins. He will try to blind you to the blessings of the gospel that have been purchased by Christ and guaranteed for you by the Holy Spirit. But remember, you are looking at your sin so you can grow, not to be punished, *because Jesus was already punished on your behalf!* It is finished. Your sin was crucified with Christ and there it remains on his cross.

Fight against the accusations of Satan by meditating on these wonderful, gospel truths:

- Your sins have been given to Christ and his righteousness has been given to you in return (2 Cor. 5:21).
- All of your past, present and future sins are forgiven by God (Col. 2:13).
- You have been reconciled to God and are now at peace with him (Rom. 5:2, 2 Cor. 5:18).
- You have been made new and have a new identity as an adopted child of God, an heir with Christ (2 Cor. 5:17, Gal. 3:29, Eph. 1:11).

In the first few weeks of removing debris from Ground Zero the construction workers discovered a tree that had been planted near the WTC plaza. It had lost most of its limbs and was badly burned. It was removed from the site and taken to an arboretum to be nursed back to health. Over the years after 9/11 that tree healed and began to grow, just as Ground Zero was transformed into a beautiful memorial plaza with new buildings springing up around it. Today that tree, which is now known as the survivor tree, stands planted in the middle of the 9/11 memorial plaza, full of new limbs and leaves.

Like the survivor tree, you and I have the same promise of new life because of the gospel. Our savior, who redeems all sin, will take the sin debris we uncover and grow us to spiritual health. So have the courage to look honestly at yourself, and, most importantly, as you do, cling tightly to the beauty of the gospel that makes you new.

Discuss It

1. Why is it so difficult to admit that we have sinned? (It's not a new problem. Take a look at Genesis 3:8.)

2. Why should we examine ourselves to identify our sin tendencies? Since the gospel promises forgiveness for our sins, what's the big deal? What does 1 John 3:4-9 say about this?

3. Hebrews 12:1 talks about "sins which cling so closely." (*The New American Standard Bible* translates this as the "sin which so easily entangles.") Think back on the past 90 days. What sins were easy for you to become entangled in? Be specific. Remember, sometimes our greatest sin struggles show up in our response to being sinned against.

4. Now, thinking about the sin(s) you shared about in question 3, write some of the consequences this sin has caused in your life. Those consequences could be emotional (fear, shame, isolation, etc.), physical (illness, injury), financial (loss of job, money, etc.), relational (loss of friendships, conflict with spouse, divorce or separation, etc.) and spiritual (lack of peace/joy, conviction, lack of intimacy with God, etc.). Also write out who was hurt by your sin. Be honest and specific.

5. As you begin the hard work of facing your sin, how is Romans 8:31-39 a consolation to you? What does this passage say about God's love for you in spite of your sin?

Summarize It:

In your own words (based on Scripture) summarize the role of self-examination in how a Christian grows into spiritual maturity.

Apply It:

Begin to spend time working in your Renew Journal examining your heart idols.

LESSON 5
OUR IDOLS

Read Scripture:
- Genesis 12:2-3
- Genesis 25:19-27:46
- Jeremiah 2:13, 3:12-13

Contemplate It:

Some of my favorite movies are from *The Lord of the Rings* trilogy. Like all great stories, *The Lord of the Rings* has echoes of the gospel, the greatest story ever written or told. Both have struggles between good and evil, sacrifice, redemption and the return of a king. And both stories end with evil finally being defeated and peace returning to the kingdom.

One of the most complicated characters in *The Lord of the Rings* is Gollum, the creature who at one moment is an ally of the hobbits (the good guys in the story) and the next moment is their enemy. Gollum's name used to be Smeagol, but that was before he came into contact with the evil ring that is at the center of the story. When Smeagol's friend discovered the ring, Smeagol wanted it for himself. So he murdered his friend. Soon all Smeagol could think about was the ring and how beautiful it was to him. He called it his *Precious*. The ring warped Smeagol's mind and turned him into a hideous creature. He began to be called Gollum and lived inside a mountain because the ring made him hate the light. That's a great picture of the effects of sin. It changes us into something awful and makes us want to live in darkness.

For Gollum, the ring became his idol. But aren't idols things like carved figures that people worship? Yes, idols include statues that are worshipped as if they were real deities, but idols are also more than that. Idols are anything that we love more than God, hoping they will meet our needs in a way that only God can. Idolatry is especially offensive to God because it is ultimately a rejection of him. Idolatry says that we value a created thing more than we value the creator, God himself. Like Gollum, something other than God becomes our *Precious*.

On its face, the story of Esau may not appear to be one of idolatry, until you read it more closely. (Read it yourself beginning at Genesis 25:19 through the end of Genesis 27.) Esau was the first born of Isaac, the son of Abraham. God had made a promise to Abraham that through him all the nations of the earth would be blessed (Gen. 12:2-3). As Abraham's grandson, Esau was part of the fulfillment of God's promise to Abraham. But in Genesis 25:29-34 we see how Esau really felt about his place in God's promise. Esau was famished from working in the field, and when he came home he saw that his brother Jacob was cooking some stew. Esau begged Jacob for a bowl. Jacob agreed to give him some stew only in return for Esau's birthright, which as the first-born son was significant. Esau would become the leader of the family and inherit most of Isaac's wealth. Most importantly, his heirs would fulfill the promise of God to Abraham. He would be part of the great lineage that produced Jesus Christ. Esau would be crazy to give this up. But he did. He said yes to Jacob and made the worst trade ever.

Why in the world would Esau do this? Can anyone really be that hungry? Verse 34 tells us why he did. It says "Esau despised his birthright." Esau was willing to make this trade not because Jacob was an especially good cook. (In fact, in Genesis 27:4 we see that Isaac actually preferred Esau's cooking.) He did it because he simply did not value what was already his—the birthright. It must have meant little to Esau. And since his birthright was wrapped up in God's promise to Abraham it was that promise which Esau really didn't value. And that is how idolatry begins every time. It starts with devaluing God and his promises to us. And when we stop valuing God and his promises (which is what worship is), we find ourselves being controlled by our flesh-driven appetites, looking for idols to serve as substitute gods. For Esau it was a silly bowl of stew. For us it could be porn, beer, work, relationships, etc. We become Gollum with something or someone as our very own *Precious*.

God, speaking through the prophet Jeremiah, says this about our idolatrous ways:

For my people have committed two evils:
they have forsaken me,
the fountain of living waters,
and hewed out cisterns for themselves,
broken cisterns that can hold no water. – Jeremiah 2:13

God says that idolatry comprises two sins. It is rejection of him (like Esau despising his birthright) and then acting like God (which is pride) by trying to meet our needs independent of God. That's the imagery of digging our own wells that Jeremiah writes about. When we chase idols we reject the fresh, flowing water that is God and instead dig a muddy well for ourselves. That's a silly trade, like exchanging an inheritance for a bowl of soup.

But God says there is another problem with our idolatrous wells. They leak. In the Middle East, where most of the Biblical story unfolds, the geology of the soil is very porous. Unless a well is lined with cement, the clean well water will leak out and mud will leak in. Jeremiah says that our idols are like broken wells. They can't hold our hope, and they won't fulfill their promises. Idolatry just doesn't work.

Because idolatry is at the root of our sins, we will begin our work of self-examination by looking for our idols. We will look for three types of idols: comfort idols (created things that we use to cope with life), control idols (behaviors that we engage in to try and control other people and our environment), and people idols (ways we look for other people to become our functional saviors or ways we seek for them to see us as their savior). We need to list the sins that go with these idols, their false beliefs that drive them, and the ways that they "leak" or fail us.

As you wrestle with your idols, do not forget God's unending love and mercy toward you. Later in Jeremiah 3:12-13, God says this:

> *"Return, faithless Israel,*
> *declares the LORD.*
> *I will not look on you in anger,*
> *for I am merciful,*
> *declares the LORD;*
> *I will not be angry forever.*
> *Only acknowledge your guilt,*
> *that you rebelled against the LORD your God"*

As we admit our sin we can know that a merciful God wants us to return to him and worship him. He wants to be our Precious.

Discuss It:

1. Jeremiah 2:13 says that idolatry comprises two aspects of sin: rejection of God and then acting like God. Looking at some of your own idolatry, in what ways do you reject God's love and seek to care for yourself apart from him.

2. What is the connection between surface sins and the deeper heart idols that fuel them? Which deeper heart idol do you struggle with the most—comfort, control, or people?

3. Esau sold his birthright (his inheritance) for stew (a temporary thrill). In what ways are your sins an exchange like Esau's—trading the eternal for a temporary thrill?

4. Jeremiah says that our idols are like cisterns that leak the water they are supposed to hold. In what ways do your idols over-promise and under-deliver?

5. Idolatry begins with devaluing the promises of God. We chase idols because at some level we do not believe that what God has promised us in the gospel is true or sufficient. In what ways do your doubts about God's promises fuel your idolatry?

Summarize It:

In your own words, summarize how the promises of God through the gospel of Jesus Christ are better than any heart idol you may be chasing. (Refer to 2 Peter 1:3, which promises that everything you need for life and godliness has already been given you in Christ.)

Apply It:

If you have not already done so, begin completing the worksheets on Heart Idols in your Renew Journal.

LESSON 6
SHAME

Read Scripture:
- Genesis 3
- Isaiah 53
- 2 Corinthians 5:17

Contemplate It:

Many of us have to wear ID badges in our workplaces. They have our pictures, names and job titles on them, and may even have the ability to electronically open locked doors. An ID badge says something about who we are and our permission to be in certain places. In other words, identity gives us access and security.

There is another kind of identity badge that is even more common. It is the badge of shame. In fact, the saying "badge of shame" really isn't just a saying. In centuries past, people who committed serious crimes were forced to wear a badge of shame, like the letter "T" branded on their forehead for acts of treason, or the letter "A" on their clothing if caught in adultery. Sadly, even the poor who did nothing wrong (apart from being born poor) would be forced to wear a badge indicating they received welfare. And many of us are aware of the most notorious badge of shame, the yellow Star of David that the Nazis forced Jews to wear (a practice they sadly borrowed from the Christian church's persecution of Jews). The point of all these "badges" would be to shun and publicly humiliate those who wore them.

Of course you and I are not forced to wear badges of shame on our clothing. But you can be sure that even if you don't wear such a badge, you do struggle with shame sometimes. All of us sinners do. Author and psychologist Ed Welch says that shame is probably at work in your life if you identify with any of these statements:

- You feel like you don't belong;
- You feel exposed; or
- You feel like there is something wrong with you[1]

I suspect every one of us have some of those feelings every week throughout the week.

So where does shame come from? Like everything else that is wrong with us and the rest of creation, shame first showed up after the fall. In fact, shame is the first consequence of sin. Before the fall, Genesis 2:25 says that Adam and Eve "were both naked and were not ashamed." Can you imagine that? Because they were in a sinless state, nothing in them felt *wrong* so they had no reason to cover up on the outside. But the fall changed that. After they sinned they knew something was wrong with them on the *inside* and that affected how they saw themselves on the outside. Adam and Eve were now aware that they were naked (Gen. 3:7), and that awareness led them to cover themselves, a symptom of the shame that was now at work in them. Not only did they cover themselves, but they also hid from God in the bushes, which is more evidence of their shame. But likely Adam and Eve's most significant moment of shame came when they were driven from the garden. Their sin made them unclean to a Holy God who cannot be in the presence of sin, so they could no longer live with him. In the story of Adam and Eve you see all of the aspects of shame at work: the sense that something is wrong with you, a feeling that you are exposed, and that you are in a place you do not belong.

If we do not deal with our shame, then it can serve as a weight that keeps us trapped in our sin. It's fuel for addiction and other destructive behaviors that we run to in order to comfort ourselves from our shame. And of course, more sin just causes more shame, which just keeps the sin/

---

[1] Ed Welch. *Shame Interrupted.* New Growth Press, 2012.

shame cycle spinning. But not only is shame fuel for sin, it can also blind us to the hope we have available to us through the gospel, a hope that we need to see clearly if we want to fight against sin. So, in many ways, shame is a huge contributor to us engaging in and remaining stuck in our sins.

But doesn't God want us to feel shame for our sins? No, God wants us to repent, not be ashamed. He brings about repentance through conviction (a sense of guilt), not shame. Whenever someone sins, that person feels guilty. Even if a person is not a believer he or she will still feel guilty for sin because his or her conscience knows the difference between right and wrong (unless that person is a psychopath). God designed us to know when we act wrongly (Rom. 2:15). But because of the sinful state we are born into, we cannot perfectly keep God's moral law (Rom. 7:18). So our repeated sin makes us feel increasing guilt, which causes our consciences to drive us to the foot of the cross where we find God's mercy.

Guilt therefore is used by God to make us desperate for salvation (and ongoing sanctification). Guilt is a good thing for us because we realize we did something wrong. Adam and Eve needed to feel guilty because they disobeyed God. *But please do not miss this next point.* If you are a believer, your guilt must not become your identity. Guilt just shows your need for the gospel; it's a diagnostic tool. If you have repented and believed in the gospel, your guilt for your sin has been transferred to Christ. You now stand blameless before God. Your disobedience says you are guilty, but grace says you are innocent![2] By remembering this good news after you sin, your conscience is freed from guilt so that you can worship God in repentance for your sin.

Like guilt, shame enters our world whenever we sin. But unlike guilt, shame attaches to us personally, not just to our

---

[2] Of course, for the unbeliever, the opposite is terrifyingly true—without the gospel you remain in your guilt and stand condemned before God. In effect, your guilt *is* your identity.

actions. Guilt says I did a bad thing. Shame says I am bad. Shame denies the truth that we are "fearfully and wonderfully made" (Ps. 139:14). Shame can also infect us even if we have been sinned against. The person who sinned against us stands guilty before God for the sin done to us, but we take on that person's guilt as our shame.

Shame also disrupts our desire to be near God and our willingness to be known by others. It isolates us and robs us of the community that we need to heal from it. We take on shame as our identity . . . it determines our self-worth. And we begin to assume that everyone around us believes the messages we believe about ourselves. This is especially true for the abused. The sexually or physically abused person internalizes the message that they are a bad person who deserves to be treated that way. Tragically, this can trap the abused person in relationships with abusers, wrongly believing they are only getting what they deserve.

Some specific sources of shame in our lives include:

- Childhood sexual and physical abuse
- Secret sins that we fear will become known
- Sins that have been seen by others that have caused us public ridicule
- Shame we take on from the sins of others that are close to us, like a family member struggling with addiction or a spouse who has been unfaithful
- Shame we feel because we do not measure up to society's expectations of beauty (such as being overweight) or success (like being unemployed)
- Shaming parents, friends, bosses, etc. who condemn us when we fail to measure up
- Cultural shame within certain ethnic groups that do not allow behaviors outside the cultural norms (such as clothing type, friendship choices, etc.)
- Religious shame that punishes and stigmatizes sin

Shame is clearly a big problem. So what hope can we have? If we go back to the story of the fall in Genesis 3 we see a hint of the hope that we need to overcome shame. Verse 21 tells us that God made clothes of animal skins for

Adam and Eve. It is a moment of grace in which God cares for Adam and Eve even in the midst of pronouncing curses on them. But this verse also foreshadows the gospel in several ways. In order for God to provide the animal skins, the animals had to die. This is the first death in a fallen creation. It is also a picture of the substitutionary death of Christ—by bearing the shame of the cross and dying to cover our sins—and the reality that apart from the shedding of blood there can be no forgiveness of sin (Hebrews 9:22). God's covering of Adam and Eve with their new clothes also points to the righteousness of Christ that covers over our sins and our shame.

The only antidote to shame is faith in the gospel. Remember, an ID badge gives us access and security. The shame badge isolates us and robs us of security. The new identity that we have through the gospel promises us that:

- Christ bore our shame so we do no longer have to (Heb. 12:2)
- Even though sin stains us, Christ makes us as white as snow (Is. 1:18)
- Because of Christ's perfect love, we no longer need live in fear (1 Jn. 4:18)
- We are a new creation; our old lives that marked us with shame have passed away (2 Cor. 5:17)
- We are part of a new family in the household of God that desires to build us up, not tear us down (Rom. 15:2)

The gospel gives us an identity badge that grants access to God in that his Spirit now lives in us (Rom. 8:11) and Christ himself intercedes for us and prays for us at the right hand of God (Rom. 8:34). And we can never lose this access. It is ours forever, guaranteed to us by God himself (Rom. 5:5).

As we continue our work of self-examination, it is important for us to take a long hard look at where shame may be present in our lives. As you completed the worksheet on self-examination from lesson 5, you likely experienced some aspects of shame as you saw your sin patterns. Spend some time this week reviewing your worksheet and highlight those sin struggles where shame seems to be the greatest.

Finally, if you are a survivor of abuse, I would encourage you to connect with a competent, Biblical counselor to begin the journey of processing through your trauma. Find someone you trust and have the courage to share your story. Let that person help you see that what happened to you was wrong, that you did not deserve it, that you have a loving savior who knows what it like to be abused, and that you can finally walk in freedom from the shame you feel.

Discuss It:

1. Which shame feeling do you identify with most and why?
   • Feeling like you do not belong
   • Feeling exposed
   • Feeling like there is something wrong with you

2. Describe some ways that shame could be contributing to your sin struggles. How does sin help comfort you in your shame or maybe serve as a way to compensate for it?

3. Thinking about your family growing up, how did shame play a role in your relationships, especially with your parents?

4. When you feel "exposed" in your sin (and shame), how do you respond? Lashing out in anger? Compensating by covering up with good behavior? Running and hiding through isolation? Other ways?

5. In what ways do you hold onto your guilt for past sins? Do you see how this is really unbelief in the gospel and evidence of shame?

Summarize It:

John 19:30 records Jesus's last words on the cross as being "It is finished." Write out in your own words how "It is finished" frees you from your guilt and shame.

Apply It:

Record in your Renew Journal some of your observations about your struggles with shame.

LESSON 7
BITTERNESS

Read Scripture:

- Job 29-31; 38-42
- Hebrews 12:1-15
- 2 Corinthians 4:16-18

Contemplate It:

I recently listened to a sermon by a pastor in which he shared about a former neighbor who was, well, just mean. She would constantly complain about her neighbors to the city government and would resist any attempts at friendship. Sadly, she was diagnosed with cancer and told that she would not live very long. So how did she choose to spend her final months? Planting trees. She planted trees all along the front of her house. When the pastor's wife made some comment about the nice gesture to plant trees that would live long after her, the neighbor promptly corrected any confusion about her real motives. She didn't plant the trees to bless others by adding beauty to the neighborhood. She planted the trees along the sidewalk so that when the trees grew larger their roots would crack the sidewalk, forcing the future owners of her home to make expensive repairs. Clearly she intended for her bitterness to live beyond the grave. Of course the Lord had the last laugh. He healed her of her sickness so she had to replace the sidewalks herself.

Many of us are just as committed to our own bitterness as that neighbor was. We spend years nursing it by thinking of all the ways we have been "wronged" by life. Maybe a dream was crushed or a spouse betrayed us. Perhaps we have lived in physical and emotional pain so long that the only thing that can come out of us is more pain. Regardless, at some point we give into the bitterness and make it the major theme of our lives.

Often an unforgiving spirit feeds our bitterness. We hold people who have harmed us in a prison that we make in our own minds. We believe that the pain they caused us is so severe that to forgive them somehow says it was ok for them to treat us that way. But the greatest irony is that we become the one imprisoned. Like the neighbor with the trees, the punishment we plan for others we end up inflicting on ourselves. As that old saying goes: "Resentment is like drinking poison and expecting the other person to die." We drink deeply from that bottle of poison and wonder why we are so miserable.

The Bible is full of examples of bitter people. Cain was bitter because the Lord rejected his sacrifice (Gen. 4:5). Saul was bitter because the Lord's favor was taken from him and given to David (1 Sam. 18:12). Job was bitter because he could not understand why God allowed his suffering (Job 9:18). Naomi was so bitter because of the deaths of her husband and sons that she wanted to be called "Mara," a Hebrew word that literally means "bitter" (Ruth 1:20). For some of these people bitterness came because of the consequences of their own sin (like Saul and Cain). For others, it was because of the difficult circumstances that came from living in a broken world (like Naomi). Regardless, their circumstances began to dominate their perspective and bitterness took over.

Scripture gives us a different picture of how to respond to life's difficulties. Here are just a few examples:

Count it all joy, my brothers, when you meet trials of various kinds – James 1:2-3

We rejoice in our sufferings – Romans 5:3

For it has been granted to you that for the sake of Christ you should not only believe in him but also suffer for his sake. – Philippians 1:29

I count everything as loss because of the surpassing worth of knowing Christ Jesus my Lord. For his sake I have suffered the loss of all things and count them as rubbish, in order that I may gain Christ. – Philippians 3:8

Share in suffering as a good soldier of Christ Jesus. – 2 Timothy 2:3

Do not repay evil for evil or reviling for reviling, but on the contrary, bless – 1 Peter 3:9

As the Lord has forgiven you, so you also must forgive. – Colossians 3:13

If you struggle with bitterness, how do you feel when you read these verses? Do you feel guilty because of your pain and therefore tempted to stuff it and act the part of the good Christian? Or maybe you even feel angry because Scripture seems to require you to respond in an impossible way to a hard situation. Should you really count it as "all joy" if your spouse cheats on you? I should rejoice in my life-threatening illness? I have to forgive the person who abused me? Really?

Yes, really. Scripture is true, authoritative and sufficient for us. So there is no getting around a biblical response to suffering and difficult circumstances. And because these are the very words of God, we must fight to believe that these teachings are also for our good. God loves us and wants us to grow and become more like Christ. So, because Christ suffered, we will suffer too. But the problem really isn't determining *what* our response should look like, but rather *how* we can have that response. How can we possibly respond to the hard stuff of life biblically?

Job experienced a series of terrible losses, all at the hands of the devil, yet still permitted by God. Early on he was able to bless the name of the Lord in the midst of his losses (Job 1:21). But as the pain piled up, eventually the bitterness did too. Things were not helped much by three friends who came to comfort Job, but instead blamed Job for his misery. Job defended himself, believing that he did not deserve what was happening to him. But both Job and his friends misunderstood what was really going on. The question was not whether Job deserved to suffer. God was allowing Job's suffering to accomplish God's objective—not to punish Job, but to glorify himself. In Job 38 God dramatically showed up in a whirlwind and then demonstrated over 125 verses how he was God and Job and his friends were not. At no point did God actually explain why he allowed Job's suffering. God simply declares his glory to Job. And then something surprising happened. Job was satisfied with God's "defense." Job admitted that he spoke about things that he did not understand, the things of God that only God knows (Job 42:3). Job then said "I had heard of you by the hearing of the ear, but now my eyes see you" (Job 42:5). Job's bitterness left him because he found God's glory in the middle of his pain. He thought he knew who God was. But because of his suffering he now gained true intimacy with God. Satan wanted Job to curse God. Instead Job worshipped God. That gives God glory.

In order for us to respond biblically to difficult circumstances and to not let a "root of bitterness" spring up in us (Heb. 12:15), we must find God's grace sufficient for us. Relying on our flesh to fight against bitterness will just make us more bitter. How do we get God's grace? Through faith. And how does faith increase in us? Through our worship. That is what Job did. He saw the glory of God and worshipped. And when we worship a glorious God, his Spirit fills us so that we can bear fruit. That's what joy is— fruit. Spiritually produced joy is a supernatural joy, not a circumstantial joy. Circumstances simply cannot account for it. Therefore, we really can "count it all joy" when we suffer (as crazy as that sounds!) because God is creating that joy in us. And as we worship God for all that he is and all that he has done for us through the gospel, we are humbled by his graciousness and can let go of the unforgiveness that we have toward others. How can we who have been forgiven so much refuse to forgive others?

In the end, we are bitter because we think more about the things that trouble us than a glorious God who loves us (Col. 3:2). That causes our circumstances to define our contentment. Freedom from bitterness comes when we worship, thinking on heavenly things, the beauty and glory of God himself and the blessings that are guaranteed to us that the temporary troubles of this world can never take away. This is what the Apostle Paul exhorted us to remember in what is perhaps the most encouraging words in Scripture, 2 Corinthians 4:16-18:

> So we do not lose heart. Though our outer self is wasting away, our inner self is being renewed day by day. For this light momentary affliction is preparing for us an eternal weight of glory beyond all comparison, as we look not to the things that are seen but to the things that are unseen. For the things that are seen are transient, but the things that are unseen are eternal.

Discuss It:

1. What difficulties in your life do you find yourself thinking about most frequently?

2. What are some unbiblical ways you respond to your difficult circumstances? Stuffing the pain and pretending everything is okay? Believing you deserve a better life than what God has given you? Blaming others? Blaming God? Medicating with comfort idols? List all the ways you are aware of.

3. In what ways do your resentments allow you to still be hurt by the people you resent? What keeps you from letting go of your resentment and forgiving them? What does your resentment say about your belief in God's sovereignty over them?

4. Read Colossians 3:1-4 and Philippians 4:4-9. Based on these Scripture, how does your thinking (what you think about, how often you think about it) affect your perspective on your difficult circumstances?

Summarize It:

Read 2 Corinthians 4:16-18 again. In your own words describe how your difficult circumstances are being used by God to prepare you for the "eternal weight of glory." How are your "momentary afflictions," as serious as they are, nothing in comparison to the hope we have in eternity. Read Ephesians 1 again to help you remember your promised inheritance.

LESSON 8
REPENTANCE PART 1:
GODLY SORROW

Read Scripture:
- 2 Samuel 11-12:15
- Psalm 51
- Romans 6:1-14

Contemplate It:

A few years ago I was traveling in Dallas for a wedding. While I know Dallas pretty well, I had never been to the area where the wedding was being held. So I loaded the destination into my GPS (this was before we had Google maps on our phones) and started driving. For a while nothing seemed wrong. I was heading in the right direction, but as time passed by I sensed there was a problem. I made one turn after another around this lake, but still could not see any signs for my destination. Then I came to a dead-end with the lake in front of me. "You have arrived at your destination" the GPS announced. Apparently the GPS had concluded that my destination was in the middle of Lewisville Lake. Since I was driving a rental car and had declined the extra insurance coverage, I opted not to drive into the lake. I backtracked to the main road and then called a friend for directions. Soon I was on my way again, but this time heading in the right direction. But the GPS kept blurting out commands to make a U-turn and head back to the middle of the lake. While the map in the GPS memory was wrong, the program in the GPS's computer was committed to it. I could either risk becoming confused and start following the GPS again, or I could turn it off and trust the new directions my friend gave me. Since the GPS had already proved it was a failure, I turned it off.

Most of us know when we are not where we want to be spiritually. If you have any doubt about that, take a look again at the work you've done in the previous three lessons examining your struggles with idols, shame and bitterness. Yet Romans 8:29 says that we have been "predestined" to become like Jesus. He's our destination. But our flesh keeps directing us away from our destination. If we expect to see any progress in our fight against sin and growth into Christlikeness then how we think about our sin has to fundamentally change. But many of us never come to a place where we desire to give up on our sin. Sure, we hate the consequences that sin causes, and we may try to engage in a few spiritual activities that we think can help us grow, but we never really come to a place where we want our sin gone. So sin keeps operating in the background, like my malfunctioning GPS, and it regularly leads us away from Christ. For real lasting change to occur, something more serious is needed. What we need is for repentance to occur.

That word repentance is a pretty loaded word for many people. If you have spent any time in church, you may associate it with a condemning style of preaching that is heavy on judgment and completely lacking of God's grace. Maybe that was the church you grew up in. Others may associate it with a character from a movie standing on a street corner carrying a sign that warns "Repent, the end is near!" Sadly, because of these stereotypes many Christians see repentance as something threatening. But nothing could be further from the truth! Repentance is actually a very hopeful word. When Jesus began his earthly ministry, he preached "Repent, for the Kingdom of Heaven is at Hand." (Matt. 5:17) Jesus wasn't threatening people with his message; it was good news! Jesus's proclamation of repentance was an invitation to give up on our failed strategies for making life work apart from God and to follow him instead.

The big idea behind repentance is to think differently about our sin. That is literally what the word repentance means—"a new way of thinking." We have to think differently about why we sin, what the payoff is, who is affected by it, and, most importantly, how our sin is ultimately an offense to God. Eve's sin in the Garden was certain once she saw that the fruit was a "delight to the eyes" so that she desired it, even though God had commanded her not to eat it (Gen. 3:16). Isn't it possible that we stay stuck in our sin because we still find it delightful and desire it? Looking at our sin honestly should bring us to a place where we want to turn away from it. In fact, we should want to run away from our sin (2 Tim. 2:2).

We have to begin to hate the sin that we see in us. Read that again—*carefully*. I am not saying hate yourself and or heap shame on yourself for your sin. Remember, Jesus's death atoned fully for your sin. *It is finished*. But you must begin to hate your sin if you ever expect to turn away from it.

The Apostle Paul wrote that in order to experience repentance, we must first have Godly sorrow for our sin. In 2 Corinthians 7:10 Paul warned that some sorrow we feel for our sin really isn't godly sorrow, but is rather worldly sorrow, a type of sorrow that keeps us trapped in the "death" of sin. Sure, we do feel sad when we have worldly sorrow, but the sadness is more about the consequences we are experiencing. Worldly sorrow usually ends when the consequences end (even if we persist in our sin). That's why we stay stuck in our sin.

King Saul is a great example of someone who had worldly sorrow. In 1 Samuel 15 Saul is confronted by the prophet Samuel for disobeying God's command to destroy the Amalekites. Saul first lied about his sin and then blamed the people of Israel for his disobedience (1 Sam. 15:21). That's what worldly sorrow does. It blames others for our sin and makes us a victim. It also makes us incredibly self-centered. Only after Samuel tells Saul that God has rejected him as king does Saul begin to use words that sound like repentance. But as the story of Saul continues through the next 16 chapters of 1 Samuel, we see that Saul just hated the consequence of his sin (the loss of his kingdom), not his sin itself. In fact, over time Saul's sin actually worsens. And because Saul never had Godly sorrow for his sin, he never repented, dying far from God with his kingdom crumbling.

Instead of worldly sorrow we should want godly sorrow for our sin. It is godly sorrow that leads to repentance (and therefore real change). Saul's successor, King David, gives us a great example of godly sorrow. In 2 Samuel 11 we read about David's adultery with Bathsheba and the murder of her husband through David's schemes. The prophet Nathan dramatically confronts David with his sin in 2 Samuel 12. David's response to Nathan is simply "I have sinned against the Lord" (2 Sam. 12:13). Well that doesn't sound very sorrowful, does it? But if you really want to know how David felt about his sin, read through Psalm 51, which he wrote after Nathan confronted him. As you read Psalm 51 you get a clear sense that David fully accepts responsibility for his sin. In Psalm 51:3-4, David says:

> For I know my transgressions, and my sin is ever before me. Against you, you only, have I sinned and done what is evil in your sight.

David *knows* his sin. He sees it clearly, even calling it evil. He knows that he has sinned against God "only." Is he minimizing his sin against Bathsheba's husband, Uriah, whom David murdered? Not at all. David knows that Uriah and Bathsheba ultimately belonged to God. His sin against them was really a sin against God. And more importantly, all of David's actions violated God's perfect law. Whenever any sin occurs God is always the one who is sinned against. That's why as you read through Psalm 51 David repeatedly begs for God's mercy. David's only hope was the grace of God because he knew that under the law his adultery was punishable by death (Lev. 20:10). Religion could not save him. David knows that his sin comes from an unclean heart that can only be changed by the cleansing work of God, not a ritualistic sacrifice (vv. 7, 10). David doesn't blame, excuse or minimize. Instead, he's broken and contrite (v.17). That's Godly sorrow and why God considered David "a man after his own heart" despite his sin (Acts 13:22).

The following chart summarizes the differences between Godly sorrow and worldly sorrow:

Godly Sorrow:	Worldly Sorrow:
• Sees sin clearly for what it is	• Minimizes and blames others
• Takes away our delight in sin	• Sorrow for consequences, not the sin
• Makes us cry out for the gospel	• Stops when the consequences do
• Makes us dead to sin (Rom. 6:11)	

Whenever we see our sin clearly, we should, like David, cry out to God for his mercy. That drives us to the cross of Jesus Christ. And there we find that the blood of Jesus cleanses us from our sin (1 Jn. 1:7). Godly sorrow never presumes upon the grace of Jesus Christ. Your sin and my sin necessitated the death of Jesus. The price paid for your sin was the "precious blood of Christ" (1 Pt. 1:19). Godly sorrow never tries to cheapen grace by assuming that our sin doesn't matter. Dietrich Bonhoffer said this:

> *Grace is costly, because it was costly to God, because it costs God the life of God's Son—"you were bought with a price"—and because nothing can be cheap to us which is costly to God. Above all, it is grace because the life of God's Son was not too costly for God to give in order to make us live. God did, indeed, give him up for us. Costly grace is the incarnation of God.*[3]

That is good news, but it should also be sobering good news. We should hate our sin for the same reason that God hates sin. Even your most petty, seemingly small sin required the death of your Savior.

---

[3] Dietrich Bonhoffer. *Discipleship.* Fortress Press, 2003

Remember it was eating forbidden fruit, not genocide, that cost us the garden. All sin is significant in the eyes of God.

Paul says that once we have believed in the gospel and been baptized, we are buried with Christ in his death and raised, like Christ, to walk in newness of life (Rom. 6:4). Because of our belief in the gospel, we should now consider ourselves dead to our sin (v.11). Do you consider yourself dead to your sin? Or is it something that you want to remain alive in you? Having a heart that wants to be dead to sin is a sign of godly sorrow.

One final word. Even if our Godly sorrow is genuine, because of our flesh our repentance is often imperfect. That is why we cling to the cross. Jesus is our only hope. Realizing that should drive us to worship Christ more and more. Which is why we not only must keep turning away from sin, but also keep turning toward God. Ultimately all sin is a reflection of our lack of worship of God. We sin because we want our sin more than we want God. We try to tell ourselves that we can love God and our sin, but that just makes us a liar (1 Jn. 4:20). Real repentance results in real worship, which is how David responded:

Deliver me from bloodguiltiness, O God,
O God of my salvation,
and my tongue will sing aloud of your righteousness.
O Lord, open my lips,
and my mouth will declare your praise. – Psalm 51:13-14

We'll look at turning toward God in worship as an act of repentance in our next lesson.

Discuss It

1. Think about the sin you are wrestling with right now. In what ways are you responding to that sin with worldly sorrow?

2. Do you have a tendency to blame others, minimize or justify your sin? How do those responses keep you stuck in your sin?

3. The Apostle Paul says that we should consider ourselves dead to our sin (Rom. 6:11). We bury things that are dead. In what ways do you allow your sin to stay alive rather than bury it?

4. The lesson said repentance means that we have to think differently about sin in light of the gospel. Go back and review the previous lessons on idols, shame, and bitterness. Based on your answers to the previous discussion questions, what are some ways that your thoughts about your sin need to change? Be as specific as you can. Are there patterns to your thoughts about your sin that keep showing up?

Summarize It:

Using Psalm 51 as a guide, write out a prayer to God in which you express sorrow for your sin. Be honest about your sin to him. Cry out for his mercy. Run to his amazing, cleansing grace. (Note: This exercise is meant to help you see your need for godly sorrow. You are not trying to convince God of what is in your heart. He already knows what is there.)

Apply It:

Record in your Renew Journal specific sinful beliefs/ thoughts and behaviors you are ready to repent of.

LESSON 9
REPENTANCE PART 2:
NEW AFFECTIONS

Read Scripture:

- Psalm 1
- 2 Timothy 3:14-17
- Philippians 4:4-9

Contemplate It:

In the previous lesson I shared about my malfunctioning GPS. If you remember, it directed me to my destination by telling me to drive into a lake. (I think it was trying to kill me.) If I was ever going to arrive at my final destination I needed to take two actions. First, I had to give up on the GPS. It had clearly failed me. Next, I had to travel in a new direction (away from the lake). Those actions are like the first steps in repentance. We have to give up on our sin by seeing it for what it really is—a destructive strategy for life that is offensive to God and required the atoning death of Christ. Clarity about our sin should lead us to godly sorrow over it. If we don't have godly sorrow about our sin, we'll still desire it and continue to pursue it.

Yet, it is not enough to simply turn away from sin. Heading in a new direction does no good if the new direction we take is still the wrong one! We need to head in the right direction—toward God. True worship always leads us back to God. Sin is fundamentally rooted in withholding our worship from God. One of the lies we tell ourselves is that we still love God even in the midst of our sin. It's a way that we minimize sin and let ourselves off the hook. Yes, it is a beautiful, gospel truth that in Christ God loves us no less when we sin. But the same cannot be said of our love for God; we love him less when we sin. Jesus commanded us to love God with all of our heart, soul and mind (Matt. 22:37). When we sin it is that sin which has captured our heart, soul and mind, not God. Repentance, therefore, is taking our misplaced worship and redirecting it back to God. Repentance is resuming our love of God.

Redirecting our worship back to God returns us to the purpose for which we were designed. St. Augustine said of God "You have made us for yourself, and our hearts are restless until we find rest in you." If we simply stop worshipping one false god, then our hearts may restlessly look for another false god to worship. That's because we fallen creatures have a tendency to trade one sin addiction for another. But false gods will never satisfy us because we were made to worship the one true God (Ex. 20:3-4). Only in Christ can we experience real rest for our souls:

> *Come to me, all who labor and are heavy laden, and I will give you rest. Take my yoke upon you, and learn from me, for I am gentle and lowly in heart, and you will find rest for your souls. For my yoke is easy, and my burden is light. – Matthew 11:28-30*

Did you ever forget to do something you wanted to do because you had too much on your mind? It happens to all of us. But it also works in reverse. What I mean is that we can actually "forget" to do something *we do not want to do* because we have too much on our minds. Worship of God crowds our minds with "things that are above, not on things that are on the earth" (Col. 3:2). Thinking about the attributes of God, his provision of the gospel, and the inheritance we have through Christ is a way to crowd out sin from our minds. We can forget to sin! That's why Paul says:

> *Finally, brothers, whatever is true, whatever is honorable, whatever is just, whatever is pure, whatever is lovely, whatever is commendable, if there is any excellence, if there is anything worthy of praise, think about these things. – Philippians 4:8*

Peter also urges something similar:

> *Therefore, preparing your minds for action, and being sober-minded, set your hope fully on the grace that will be brought to you at the revelation of Jesus Christ. As obedient children, do not be conformed to the passions of your former ignorance, but as he who called you is holy, you also be holy in all your conduct, since it is written, "You shall be holy, for I am holy." – 1 Peter 1:13-16*

Both Paul and Peter tell us to bring our thoughts to worshipful things about God. Thoughts about God and his provision of grace through Christ lead us to think Godly, so that we desire to be Godly, not sinful. Thomas Chalmers, a 19th century pastor in Scotland, described this as the "expulsive power of a new affection." Our affection for God displaces our affection for sin.

So let's get very practical. In Lesson 3 we learned about means of grace, which we described as sprinklers that watered our dry souls. Means of grace strengthen our faith so that we can tap into the power of God to fight against sin. As discussed above, if we desire to turn toward God in worship then we have to direct our minds to think about God, not our desire to sin. How do we do that? We need to use God's chosen means of grace to shape our thoughts: meditation on Scripture. When we read Scripture we are reading the very words of God (2 Tim. 3:16). So, if we want to follow the advice of 1 Peter 1:13-16 and have holy thoughts that lead to holy conduct, then we must meditate on God's holy words.

What does it mean to meditate on God's word? In order to meditate on Scripture, we first have to read Scripture, which for many of us is the hardest part. But once we read it and understand what it means, we can then move on to meditation, where we linger over it and continue to bring it back to our minds. In Dr. Donald Whitney's book *Spiritual Disciplines* he encourages using Philippians 4:8 as a guide for meditation on Scripture. When you meditate on

Scripture Dr. Whitney encourages asking these questions about the passage you are meditating on:

- What is true about this, or what truth does it exemplify?
- What is honorable about this?
- What is just or right about this?
- What is pure about this, or how does it exemplify purity?
- What is lovely about this?
- What is commendable about this?
- What is excellent about this (that is, excels others of this kind)?
- What is praiseworthy about this?

After we spend time in meditation we then simply pray back to God what we learned from our meditation. We praise him for his excellence and give him the glory that he alone is due. If your meditation has made you aware of some sin, then confess that to God and thank him for the free gift of salvation that you have in Jesus Christ.

Remember our definition of repentance from last week: To repent is to have a new way of thinking. We think differently by turning our thoughts away from the destructiveness of sin and toward the beauty of God. Meditation and prayer are means of grace that shape our thoughts toward God. And when we think about the holiness of God, we don't desire to live in our sin but instead to be holy like him.

Discuss It:

1. Think about the sin you struggle with most often. How often do think about and act out in that sin? Compare those actions with how often you think about God and engage in activities that make you more mindful of him. What is the connection here with repentance?

2. Think about how worship of God was described in this lesson. How does that compare to your understanding of worship?

3. In previous lessons we discussed the need for God's grace to fuel our efforts to change. God's grace comes to us through our faith. What is the connection between worship and faith?

4. Do you have a rhythm of following daily spiritual practices like Scripture reading and prayer? How do these practices shape your thought patterns? If you do not have a daily rhythm for spiritual practices, what keeps you from starting?

Summarize It:

Write out a prayer of praise to God. Include qualities of God that you find worshipful. If you are struggling with where to begin, read through passages of Scripture to remind you of who God says he is. Some passages you could read through include Job 38-39, the Psalms (try any of Psalms 120 to 134), Romans 8:31-39, Ephesians 2:1-10, 3:14-21, Philippians 2:1-11, and Colossians 1:15-23.

Apply It:

Record in the Repentance section of your Renew Journal specific ways your affection for God is growing.

LESSON 10
REPENTANCE PART 3: MAKING PEACE

Read Scripture:
- Matthew 5:21-26
- Luke 19:1-10
- Colossians 3:12-17

Contemplate It:

The world has seen much misery since the fall of man in the Garden of Eden, but there is little comparison to the extreme, concentrated horror that occurred for three months in 1994 in the country of Rwanda. From early April though mid-July of that year, over 800,000 Rwandans were murdered by their neighbors, friends, co-workers, and sadly, even their pastors. The ruling ethnic group, the Hutus, were trying to wipe out another ethnic group, the Tutsis, with whom they had been engaged in a civil war for years. By the time it was over, 70% of the Tutsis and 20% of the total population of Rwanda lay dead. The genocide stopped only after Tutsi rebels took control of the country.

If the story of Rwanda followed the typical pattern of ethnic conflict, the new Tutsi government would have engaged in systematic retribution against the Hutus. But what happened next in Rwanda was not typical. Many Hutus who committed the genocide were imprisoned, but the new government's judicial system was soon overwhelmed, with some estimating that it would take up to 400 years to bring everyone to trial. Besides that, the government also knew that punishment of the guilty alone would never heal their country. So the government, with the help of leading Rwandan Christians, began to promote a process whereby those who were guilty confessed their crimes and the families of the victims forgave them. It was the sort of reconciliation preached by Jesus, but on a national scale. Tens of thousands of Hutus have now confessed their crimes and many thousands of Tutsis have forgiven them. How is this possible?

Apart from the work of God's grace in our hearts, we cannot do seemingly impossible things like forgive the person who murdered members of our family. In fact, that is the whole point of the gospel. If the things of God depended on man, they would never come to pass. But as Jesus pointed out "with God all things are possible" (Matt. 19:26).

Ultimately God himself does for us what he requires of us. Too many of us read the kingdom teachings of Jesus (like the Sermon on the Mount) as things we are "supposed to do." But Jesus is building his kingdom, not you or me. Yes, when Jesus is in control of our hearts, we begin to desire that his kingdom would actually come and that his will would be done, on earth as it is in heaven. But don't miss the point that in the Lord's Prayer (Matt. 6:10), Jesus wants us to pray for God's kingdom to come because he knew that its coming depended on God, not on his disciples. God may use us to achieve his purposes, like reconciliation between enemies, but it is always God who is making it come to pass. He is in control. We are just the means he uses.

A sign that you are repentant for your sin is that you will become an ambassador of God's peace (2 Cor. 5:20) and seek to be reconciled with those you have harmed through your sin. Again, being at peace with someone else is not what gives you peace with God. Instead, the fact that you are at peace with God through the gospel should create a desire in you for that peace to be in all your relationships. You will feel a sense of urgency to be reconciled with everyone. So repentant people take the initiative to be reconciled. That's the point of Jesus's teaching in Matthew 5:23-24:

If you are offering your gift at the altar and there remember that your brother has something against you, leave your gift there before the altar and go. First be reconciled to your brother, and then come and offer your gift.

According to this passage, taking the initiative to be at peace even has priority over your worship. God sees mending you fractured relationships as that important!

In many cases where reconciliation is needed, responsibility for the fractured relationship can be found on both sides. And this is where reconciliation often gets sidetracked. We have a tendency to make our efforts to be reconciled conditioned upon the other person first taking responsibility for their wrongs done to us. But that thinking is not in step with the gospel. We are not the other person's Holy Spirit and have no right to make them do anything. That is God's role, which is why Paul says: "If possible, so far as it depends on you, live peaceably with all." (Rom. 12:18) Even if the other person never takes responsibility for their sin against us, a repentant posture toward our own sin should compel us to take responsibility for what we did wrong. That's the part of reconciliation that depends on us. If you recall Psalm 51:3, David said he knew *his* transgressions and that *his* sin was always in front of him. David's words reflect the humility that comes with true repentance; you become so aware of your own sin that you do not have the desire to look for sin in others.

Believing in the gospel gives us humility about our sin, but it also frees us to reject our idolatry and embrace the kingdom of Christ as our true home. Colossians 1:13 states that through the gospel we have literally been transferred from the domain of darkness (where Satan rules) to the kingdom of the beloved son, Jesus Christ. The benefits of this new kingdom free us to let go of our need to defend ourselves, win an argument, keep possessions, and protect our reputation, which often hinder our efforts at reconciliation. If we are repentant, we no longer need to keep up appearances. The gospel frees us to not hold back in our attempts at reconciliation with others because we already have the most precious thing ever—the Kingdom of God!

The story of Zacchaeus in Luke 19:1-10 demonstrates gospel belief empowering extravagant steps toward reconciliation. Zacchaeus was a tax collector. For many of us, tax collectors bring to mind thoughts of the IRS, but in fact tax collectors like Zacchaeus were hated much more than the IRS is today. Zacchaeus collected taxes for the Romans, so he helped finance the occupation of Israel by the Roman legions. He was a collaborator with the enemy. If you were a Jew and a family member had been killed by a Roman soldier, then you would likely blame tax collectors as much as the Romans. But beyond collaborating with the Romans, tax collectors were also hated because they abused their offices by overcharging taxpayers. Tax collectors bid for the right to collect taxes, and they were entitled to keep as profit anything more than what they collected for Rome. Zacchaeus and other tax collectors became rich by, in effect, stealing from their neighbors.

Those of us who grew up in the church may only remember Zacchaeus because of the children's song about him being a "wee little man" who climbed up in a sycamore tree to see Jesus. (Seriously, if you have never heard the song, Google it.) Zacchaeus' desire to seek Jesus was so strong that he went to embarrassing lengths to see him. But what is more amazing about the story is what happened next: Jesus went home with Zacchaeus, a notorious sinner! And while Scripture does not say exactly what transpired at Zacchaeus' house, Jesus himself declared that salvation came to Zacchaeus that day.

Zacchaeus was so transformed by his encounter with Jesus that people became more important to him than his riches. First, he decided to give half of his possessions to the poor. But he also promised to restore the money he had defrauded, fourfold. This meant that for those from whom he had stolen the equivalent of $100 he would pay back $400! Under the law, Zacchaeus was certainly obligated to pay back what he stole, plus a 20% fine (Lev. 6:5; Num. 5:6-7), but because he experienced the riches of Jesus's extravagant grace he desired to do more than simply "go through the motions" of reconciliation. He wanted real reconciliation, regardless of what it cost him.

Many times I have seen attempts at reconciliation fail because the person apologizing and making amends for a sin did not have godly sorrow nor a desire to see real reconciliation occur. Instead it seemed they were just checking a box because a pastor or counselor told them they needed to apologize. That will never lead to true reconciliation.

Worship for how much God has done for us in Jesus will free us to pursue real reconciliation. That's what happened to Zacchaeus. Repentance and belief in the gospel gives us the courage to actually care about how someone has been affected by our sin because our focus is now off ourselves and on God and others. It is an amazing moment of reconciliation when one sinner says to another "I have sinned against you by doing _____. This was completely my fault. If you feel comfortable doing so, I want to hear how my sin has hurt you." When the gospel empowers reconciliation conversations like this real healing occurs and God is glorified (because his grace brought the reconciliation about).

Finally, we can be ambassadors of peace when we choose to forgive someone who has sinned against us. Colossians 3:13 says that "if one has a complaint against another, [forgive] each other; as the Lord has forgiven you, so you also must forgive." Some of us need to grant forgiveness for truly horrendous things that have been done to us . . . things like betrayal and terrible acts of physical, emotional or sexual abuse. How can we forgive that? Again, in our flesh, it is impossible, but through God's grace all things are possible. Perhaps reconciliation need be no more than granting forgiveness and surrendering the person who hurt you to God. If that person is unrepentant and perhaps even a danger, that is all you need do. Resuming a relationship in that situation may not be wise. Get help from a biblical counselor or pastor to understand what Scripture teaches in your specific circumstances. The main thing is to let go of your unforgiveness and embrace your own need for the gospel. Unforgiveness is more of a burden than you were meant to carry. For most of us though, the person who hurt us is not abusive or dangerous and the relationship can be truly restored if you become willing to forgive that person. Will you do that?

A decade after the genocide, *Christianity Today* reported on the efforts at national reconciliation in Rwanda.[4] The article shared a story about a Hutu Christian who came to a Tutsi Christian to ask for forgiveness. The Tutsi woman, who lived through the genocide, hated Hutus. Then the Lord began to work on her heart. She felt the Lord saying to her "All those times you said you wanted to kill a Hutu, are you not the same as him?" The article goes on to say:

> *The [Tutsi] woman began weeping, raced back to her room, and grabbed a new skirt. Minutes later, she saw [the Hutu] and put the skirt at his feet. "Here is a Tutsi woman giving you forgiveness and asking your forgiveness for the way she looked at Hutu. Put this skirt in your bathroom. When you and your wife and children come out of the shower, I want you to wipe your feet on it and remember this Tutsi woman who often killed Hutus in her thoughts. Please forgive me."*

Like Zacchaeus, this Tutsi woman had an extravagant moment of grace where the Lord showed her the sin in her own heart. The love of Jesus humbled her in that moment so that she could give an extravagant act of forgiveness to the Hutu man. This is what the gospel is all about—God's extravagant grace empowering us to love in an extravagant way, all to the praise of his glorious name.

---

[4] "Forgiveness 101." *Christianity Today*. April 2004. p. 13.

Discuss It:

1. In what ways do you struggle with comparing your sins to the sins of others? Do you use the sins of others to avoid taking responsibility for the ways you have sinned against them?

2. What steps can you take today to be reconciled with these people?

3. What are some of the conditions you attach to forgiving someone? How does your conditional forgiveness compare to God's unconditional forgiveness of you?

4. What is preventing you from forgiving these people right now? If you are unwilling to forgive them, ask God to soften your heart toward them.

Summarize It:

In your own words, describe how the blessings we have in the gospel free us to take responsibility for our sin, regardless of what it may cost us in terms of resources or reputation.

Apply It:

Record in your Renew Journal the names of the people you need to forgive and those from whom you need to ask forgiveness and make peace.

LESSON 11
CONNECTING THE DOTS

Read Scripture:

- 2 Peter 1:3-11
- 1 Timothy 3:6-10
- Philippians 2:1-13

Contemplate It:

Did you ever draw pictures as a child by "connecting-the-dots?" The object was to draw a line from dot to dot following a numerical sequence. Once all the dots were connected, a picture would emerge. For many of us, that game was the only way we could draw a picture. (At least that was true for me.) While the pictures we might have "drawn" as children were quite simple, the connect-the-dot method can also be used to draw more intricate pictures. In fact, connect-the-dot activity books are available for adults too, allowing you to draw art by masters such as Rembrandt and Leonardo Da Vinci. Yes, you can even use connect-the-dots to sketch the Mona Lisa. All you need to do is follow the pattern that has been laid out for you.

Over the course of this study we have laid out many of the "dots" that are components of God's process for change. Now it's time to step back and look at the picture that has emerged. By now we should have a growing awareness of the many ways that sin is at work in our lives. That awareness should strip us of our self-confidence that we can change ourselves. If we have any doubts, just look at our repeated cycles of trying hard on our own to change, followed by failure, shame, more sin, more trying hard, etc. Our awareness of the power of sin at work in us will make us desperate and drive us to the cross of Jesus Christ. It is the desperateness caused by sin and the joy found in Christ that made Paul write in Romans 7:24-25:

> *Wretched man that I am! Who will deliver me from this body of death? Thanks be to God through Jesus Christ our Lord!*

At the cross we find not only the comfort of God's forgiving grace, but we also receive the power of God's transforming grace that fuels our efforts to fight against sin. Just like our initial trusting faith in Christ at salvation brings forgiveness for our sins and reconciles us to God, our ongoing trusting faith in Christ also brings a filling of the Holy Spirit who lives in us and fights for us to overcome our sin. That's what grace does: It gives life to us and fights for us. So, the biblical prescription for change is to repent of sin, believe in the gospel, and receive the grace that empowers the Christian life.

Hopefully your awareness of sin and the abundance of God's grace to fight against that sin are resulting in real growth into Christlikeness. But how do you continue to grow over the long-term? Many people start out strong with a genuine desire to grow and fight against sin, but at some point they fall away and revert back to old patterns. Why does that happen?

If we are not experiencing sustained spiritual growth, then we must ask ourselves if we truly desire to turn away from our sin (repent) and whether we really believe that God will give us his power to overcome that sin (2 Cor. 9:8, 12:9). No doubt, we will have failures in our fight against sin. That is the difficult reality of living in a fallen world with sin still alive in us. When failure occurs, we must reject the shame that the enemy heaps on us, and instead cling closer to Christ, knowing that in him God is fully pleased with us despite our many failures. But if we are not seeing some growth in our fight against sin, then we have to be honest with ourselves and admit there is something wrong with what we believe about sin, the gospel or both. The Apostle Peter says that we fall back and stumble because we have allowed ourselves to become "nearsighted" and "blind" and forgotten all that we have received through the gospel (2 Pt. 1:9).

Those who continue to grow into Christlikeness are not blind to their ongoing need for the gospel. In fact, growth in the Christian life is measured by increasing dependence on God's grace, not independence from him. Does that mean we are passive and simply sit back and let God do all the work? Absolutely not! We engage in much personal effort because there is a discipline that comes with the pursuit of personal holiness. Consider these verses:

- I discipline my body and keep it under control. – 1 Cor. 9:27
- Make every effort to supplement your faith with virtue, and virtue with knowledge, and knowledge with self-control, and self-control with steadfastness, and steadfastness with godliness, and godliness with brotherly affection, and brotherly affection with love. – 2 Peter 1:5-7
- Only let your manner of life be worthy of the gospel of Christ, so that whether I come and see you or am absent, I may hear of you that you are standing firm in one spirit, with one mind striving side by side for the faith of the gospel. – Philippians 1:27
- Train yourself for godliness; for while bodily training is of some value, godliness is of value in every way, as it holds promise for the present life and also for the life to come. – 1 Timothy 4:7-8
- Therefore, my beloved, as you have always obeyed, so now, not only as in my presence but much more in my absence, work out your own salvation with fear and trembling, for it is God who works in you, both to will and to work for his good pleasure. – Philippians 2:12-13

What is the effort that we engage in? That's right: Repent (of our sins) and believe (in the gospel). The pattern for the Christian life is to discipline ourselves to look for sin, confess it, repent of it, and believe once again that everything we need for life and godliness has been given to us in Christ through the gospel. And what does that discipline look like on the ground, day to day? Just like when you go to the gym and engage in different exercises to "shape" your body, we engage in spiritual disciplines so that God can shape our souls. We train ourselves for godliness through:

- Study and meditation on Scripture so that our thoughts are shaped by the thoughts of God, rather than having them shaped by a culture under the control of the devil;
- Prayer and worship throughout the day so that our thought patterns are being redirected toward God rather than toward idols or circumstances that make us anxious;
- Practicing self-examination so that we see where sin and unbelief are present and God's transforming grace is needed;
- Confessing our sins regularly so that we do not fall into self-deception and the hardness of sin;
- Placing ourselves under the authority of a local church and someone mature in the faith to disciple us and provide biblical counsel when needed.

These disciplines and many others must become a new pattern for living. They do not create holiness in us. Only God's grace does that. But they do make us aware of our need for, and the abundant provision of, that grace. And this pattern is not something we run to just when we are in a struggle. It has to become the pattern for our everyday lives. If this study simply becomes something you complete and then move on from, quite likely whatever sin struggles you had before the study will return some day (probably very soon). But if you are able to adopt a new pattern of daily living where you regularly practice the disciplines and focus on your ongoing need to repent and believe, then you will begin to "connect-the-dots" in a new way. You will see a new picture beginning to emerge—a picture of you becoming like Christ.

Discuss It:

1. Have you ever committed to "turning over a new leaf" and changing, only to give up on it within a short time? What caused you to give up?

2. On a typical day, how much time do you spend pursuing spiritual disciplines? What is the greatest obstacle to you devoting more time to them? Do you doubt they make much of a difference?

3. Think about the significant sin struggle that is the tornado in your life you shared about in Lesson 1. How much time do you spend most days thinking, planning, and acting out in that sin? How could you take that time and spend it with God instead?

4. In what ways do you still struggle with believing the gospel?

Summarize It:

In your own words, describe your role and God's role in your pursuit of personal holiness. (Read Philippians 2:12-13 again if you need help.)

Apply It:

Record in the Renew Journal your personal plan for regularly practicing spiritual disciplines.

LESSON 12
STORIES OF GRACE

Read Scripture:
- Book of Ruth
- Acts 25-26
- 1 Peter 3:15

Contemplate It:

You can tell a lot about someone's journey in life by looking at his or her music and movie collections. For example, my music library reflects the somewhat meandering path my life has taken over the past thirty years of adulthood. You'll find a fair amount of classic rock from high school, 80's alternative rock from my college years (think early R.E.M. and U2), some campy stuff like Sinatra, Dean Martin, and the Bee Gees (don't judge me) and a fair amount of classical music, hymns and liturgical chants. Yep, it's a strange journey I have been on.

My movie collection is a little narrower in its focus though. I'm a big fan of *The Lord of the Rings, Star Wars, Harry Potter* and *Band of Brothers*. Beyond telling you I am a guy, my movie library says something else about me. It says that I love stories of struggle where the main characters are in a fight against the forces of darkness. Sound familiar?

In the second book of the *Lord of the Rings* trilogy (*The Two Towers*), Sam the hobbit says to his traveling companion and fellow hobbit Frodo "I wonder what sort of a tale we've fallen into?" That's a great question for you and me to wrestle with too. In looking at the story of our lives, what sort of tale have *we* fallen into? Is it a tragedy where the hero deserves to win but doesn't? Or is it a morality tale where the hero overcomes hardship through great personal effort?

Actually, it's neither. The story we have fallen into is a much bigger story than we realize. It is the story of God's redemptive work within human history to bring about his sovereign plans. "Redemptive" is the key word in that sentence. In a redemptive story, someone needs to be rescued (or redeemed) from a difficult set of circumstances. The rescuer is the hero in a redemptive story, not the person in need of rescue. So, in our story, we are the ones in need of rescue, and the rescuer is Jesus Christ.

But we do not like to see ourselves as weak and in need of rescue, do we? Matt Chandler, lead pastor of The Village Church, says that we love to read the story of David and Goliath and see the point of the story as "be like David and kill the giants in your life." But since we know that Jesus is ultimately the hero of all biblical stories, the shepherd-future king David really must point us to the better, sinless shepherd-king Jesus. Do you want to find yourself in the story of David and Goliath? Matt says we are really Israel hiding in our tent afraid that Goliath will kill us! (Ouch.)

The Book of Ruth is a great story of redemption. It's a book that you can read in a short amount of time. At the beginning of the story, Naomi's husband and two sons die. Her daughter-in-law Ruth travels with her back to Naomi's hometown, Bethlehem. The way that Ruth cared for her mother-in-law was exemplary, and it would be easy to see the point of the story as "be kind, like Ruth." But that's not the point. Because Naomi and Ruth did not have husbands, they really had no place in society and were in danger of starving to death. Only because of the mercy of a distant relative of Naomi, Boaz, did they survive. Boaz allowed Ruth to pick grain from his fields. Later in the story we see Boaz purchasing land in which Naomi's dead husband had rights. He did this not only to redeem the land for Naomi's family but to also gain the right to marry Ruth. And who is in the line of descendants of Boaz and Ruth? Both King David (Ruth 4:22) and King Jesus (Matt. 1:5, Lk. 3:32).

Boaz became Ruth's gracious redeemer by paying for the land that belonged to Naomi's family. We see God working redemptively in the story of Ruth in that he took a tragedy (the death of Naomi's husband and sons) and used it to accomplish his saving purposes in the world (by creating a line of descendants that included David and Jesus.) Boaz's redeeming actions should also remind us of our redemption by Jesus. Christ redeems us through his death on the cross by purchasing the grace that sets us free from God's wrath and adopting us into his new covenant family (Gal. 4:5).

So what's the whole point of focusing on the redemptive story? It determines how we read Scripture and how we understand life. As Tim Keller says, we will either read Scripture through the grid of what we must do or through the grid of what God has already done. Reading Scripture through the lens of redemption means that we read Genesis through Revelation by asking "how does this point to my need for Christ" and "how does this reassure me of all that Christ has done for me." In other words, all of Scripture is about gospel need and gospel provision.

Reading Scripture through a redemptive lens will also change how we understand and share our own stories. Too many Christians reduce their testimonies to a dry statement about the dates of their conversion and baptism, or worse, they make it a resume listing all of their religious activities. It is the rare exception to hear a testimony in which someone shares about his or her weaknesses, moral failures and need for God's redeeming grace. I had a friend who had a significant moral failure, but God's grace changed him and brought healing to his marriage. Yet he struggled with sharing about his failure. He wanted to be like "normal" Christians who did not talk openly about their sin struggles. But isn't God's glorious grace at work in our lives the very thing we should be talking the most about?

The testimony that Paul gives before Agrippa in Acts 26 is a great illustration of sharing your story in a redemptive way. Paul does not hold back in sharing his awful sins in persecuting and murdering the first Christians. Why?

Because his sin brought him face to face with Jesus on the road to Damascus. He doesn't brag about his sin, but he shares it so that he can boast more about Jesus. This is a pattern that Paul follows throughout his letters where he shares his weaknesses so that he can boast about Jesus. It is a pattern that we can follow too.

So who needs to hear about God's redeeming work in your life? You do! We need to constantly remind ourselves that the good news of the gospel at work in our lives is way more powerful than sin at work in our lives. As you see your sin, remind yourself of all that God has already done for you through Christ. Jerry Bridges called this preaching the gospel to yourself:

> *To preach the gospel to yourself, then, means that you continually face up to your own sinfulness and then flee to Jesus through faith in His shed blood and righteous life. It means that you appropriate, again by faith, the fact that Jesus fully satisfied the law of God, that He is your propitiation, and that God's holy wrath is no longer directed toward you.*[5]

Preaching the gospel to yourself helps you see God's redemptive work in your life. It changes your perspective from one of shame and defeat to one of hope. That's why Peter tells us to honor Christ in our hearts. To honor Christ means that we worship him for all that he has, is and will do. That fills us with hope. And when we are filled with hope, what we share with others is the genuine hope that is in us (1 Pt. 3:15)!

Remember, life is not about you or me. It is about God. He is the point to the story, and he is always the hero of the story. Never run away from sharing about your sin struggles. Instead, boast that in spite of your sin, God is doing wondrous things in you. That's why my life verse is 1 Cor. 15:10a: "But by the grace of God I am what I am, and his grace toward me was not in vain."

---

[5] Jerry Bridges. *The Discipline of Grace.* NavPress, 2006.

Discuss It

1. How do you see your own story? A tragedy (you deserved to "win" but didn't), a morality tale (you deserved to win and did), or a redemptive story (God won for you)?

2. How do you tend to apply Scripture when you read it? As tragedy, morality, or redemption? For example, in Mark 12:30-31, Jesus commands us to love God with all our heart, soul, mind and strength and to love our neighbors as ourselves (which is essentially a restatement of the Ten Commandments). A "tragic" application would say this is impossible, so why try? A "moralistic" application would say that we can obey this command in our own strength, if we try. A "redemptive" application says that all of the commands of God have been fulfilled in Christ and his obedience is credited to those who believe in the gospel.

3. When you think about your sin, do you feel shame or gratitude for what Jesus has done to redeem your sin?

4. Romans 8:28 says "And we know that for those who love God all things work together for good, for those who are called according to his purpose." This is not a promise that things will work out according to our plans, but that God will accomplish his purposes in spite of our sin. In what ways do you see God redeeming your sin to accomplish something good?

Summarize It:

Take an opportunity to preach the gospel to yourself. Share why you need the gospel (get specific) and how through

Christ God has graciously redeemed you and is making you new.

Apply It:

Record in the Renew Journal how you may already see God redeeming your sin.

CONCLUSION

Quite often individuals go through a Bible study and experience a new-found excitement in their spiritual life. I pray that has been true for you in this study. But there is a challenge that we all must acknowledge. Often within just a few short weeks after completing a Bible study the excitement subsides and we fall back into old patterns of living. Will anything be different this time?

Here are some things to keep in mind as you continue the journey of growing up in the faith:

1. The key to long-term growth is to remember what we have stressed so often in this study—the gospel! Never stop marveling at all that has been, is being, and will be done for you through Christ Jesus. Keep pondering the tremendous blessings catalogued in Ephesians 1 that are yours through faith in the gospel!

2. In 2 Corinthians 4:16, Paul reassures us that "though our outer self is wasting away, our inner self is being renewed day by day." The journey of renewal is indeed day by day. Every day we need to repent of the ways we have denied the Gospel and once again believe in it. That is the discipline that leads to growth over the long-term. All the lessons in this study can serve as a template to incorporate into your daily spiritual routine—examine yourself, long for godly sorrow for your sin, repent (by hating your sin and loving God), and take steps to forgive those who have sinned against and make amends to those you have sinned against. These actions on their own do not accomplish your renewal (God does that for us), but they do serve to strengthen our faith and

help us fight against our flesh. That is the role we play in our sanctification.

3. Share what you have learned in this study with others, perhaps even leading a group through the study yourself. The essence of discipleship is simply to share with others what has been taught to you – that's what 2 Timothy 2:2 teaches. Be a disciple of Jesus who makes disciples of Jesus. And what I have found personally true is that as I teach others about the gospel, my own understanding of the gospel grows.

Congratulations on finishing this study. I pray that it has deepened your love for Christ and made you want to grow to be more like him.

RENEW JOURNAL

The Renew Journal is meant to serve as a guide to help you examine your inner and outer life—your beliefs, thoughts, priorities, actions and relationships. The objective of this examination of yourself is to see the sin patterns that are at work in your life and the effects they have on you and those around you. Where these sin patterns are present is also where God's grace is needed to change you. Take the time to work in the journal throughout our study. This is where you will take the ideas we teach on and discuss in our small groups and apply them to your own life and specific sin struggles.

It would also be wise to meet with two or three others in your small group as you work through the journal to share your answers with one another and to encourage each other in the gospel. If you get stuck, don't quit! Speak with your small group leader who may be able to help you get going again.

Facing the Hard Facts About Your Sin
Complete After Lesson 1

After a tornado moves through an area, a team of experts from the weather service will go through the area that was hit to assess the damage. Based on the degree of destruction the experts will then rate the severity of a storm.

Change is very hard even with the best motivation. But change is absolutely impossible if we are not yet convinced of the need for change in our lives. Spend some time meditating on Psalm 139:23-24: "Search me, O God, and know my heart. Try me and know my thoughts! And see if there be any grievous way in me, and lead me in the way everlasting!" Then review the list of consequences on each page. Check each box beside the consequences you have experienced.[6]

Now take a look at your "damage report." In what ways do you still feel like your sin struggle is not that serious? How are you minimizing it? Do you believe that you can change on your own?

Emotional Consequences
- ☐ Attempted suicide
- ☐ Suicidal thoughts/feelings
- ☐ Homicidal thoughts/feelings
- ☐ Feelings of extreme hopelessness of despair
- ☐ Failed efforts to your behavior or the behavior of others
- ☐ Feeling like two people— one public, one private
- ☐ Emotional instability (depression, paranoia, fear of going insane)

---

[6] Adapted from *A Gentle Path through the Twelve Steps: The Classic Guide for All People in the Process of Recovery* by Patrick J. Canres, PhD. (Hazelden Publishing, 1993).

☐ Loss of touch with reality

☐ Loss of self-esteem

☐ Loss of life goals

☐ Acting against your own values and beliefs

☐ Strong feelings of guilt and shame

☐ Isolation and loneliness

☐ Fears about the future

☐ Other emotional consequences (specify):_____
_____
_____
_____
_____
_____

Physical Consequences

☐ Continuation of behavior that risks your health

☐ Extreme weight loss or gain

☐ Physical problems (e.g., ulcers, high blood pressure)

☐ Physical injury or abuse by others

☐ Involvement in potentially abusive or dangerous situations

☐ Vehicle accidents

☐ Self-abuse or injury

☐ Sleep disturbances

☐ Physical exhaustion

☐ Other physical consequences (specify):_____
_____
_____
_____

_____
_____

Spiritual Consequences

☐ Strong feelings of spiritual emptiness

☐ Feeling disconnected

☐ Feeling abandoned by God

☐ Anger at God

☐ Loss of faith in God

☐ Cessation of church activities

☐ Other spiritual consequences (specify):_____
_____
_____
_____
_____

Family Consequences

☐ Risking the loss of spouse

☐ Loss of spouse

☐ Increase in marital or relationship problems

☐ Jeopardizing the well-being of your family

☐ Loss of your family's respect

☐ Increase in problems with your children

☐ Loss of family of origin

☐ Other family consequences (specify):_____
_____
_____

_____

_____

_____

☐ Stealing

☐ Other
(specify):_____

_____

_____

_____

_____

_____

_____

____

Career and Educational Consequences

☐ Decrease in productivity at work

☐ Demotion at work

☐ Loss of co-workers' respect

☐ Loss of career of your choice

☐ Failing grades in school

☐ Loss of educational opportunities

☐ Loss of business

☐ Forced to change careers

☐ Underemployed

☐ Termination from job

☐ Other career and educational consequences
(specify):_____

_____

_____

_____

_____

_____

Other Consequences

☐ Loss of important friendships

☐ Loss of interest in hobbies or activities

☐ Few friends

☐ Financial problems

☐ Illegal activities

☐ Court or legal involvement

☐ Lawsuits

☐ Prison

Believing the Gospel
Complete After Lesson 2

In what ways do you doubt your need for the gospel, either by minimizing your sin or by seeing the problem in your life (whatever it is) as being something you can fix on your own?

In what ways do you doubt whether the gospel is a practical help to you?

How does your view of God hinder your ability to believe that the gospel is good news for you?

Spotting Your the Patterns
Complete After Lesson 3

When we are living in our flesh there are noticeable patterns in our thoughts, emotions and behaviors. Seeing those patterns are key to knowing what needs to change in us. Romans 8:5 says that thoughts focused on our flesh will produce a life that is corrupted by the flesh. Take a few minutes and think about what you think about when you are struggling in your sin, then answer the below questions.

When you are struggling the most with sin, what emotional state are you usually in? (The focus here is not on the emotions that result from your sin, but the emotions that set you up to sin.) Are you depressed, sad, lonely, fearful, angry, feeling out-of-control, etc.?

What life circumstances or environmental conditions create a temptation for you to sin? This could include travel, family strife, work difficulties, financial set-backs, etc.

What do you feel after you engage in your sin struggles? How does your past sin set your emotional state up for a future sin?

Heart Idols
Complete As You Work on Lesson 4 and 5

1. The next several pages consist of worksheets that list sin struggles falling into three different categories of heart idols: **comfort idols** (ways we look to created things to make us feel secure or to relieve anxiety), **control idols** (ways we seek to act like God by exercising control over other people or our circumstances), and **people idols** (ways we look for other people to become our functional saviors or ways we seek for them to see us as their savior).

2. It starts by listing the sins that are commonly associated with each heart idol. Don't be overwhelmed! Not everyone will struggle with every sin listed on the worksheets. If a sin doesn't pertain to you, simply skip it.

3. If you do struggle with one of the sins listed, for "Your Behavior" write in some basic information about that struggle. Include things like frequency and some of the types of behaviors that go with the sin. You do not need to try and list out every time you engaged in this sin. However, if a specific example will help you see the destruction better, then describe that event.

4. Next, for "Driving Belief," describe your beliefs and feelings that drive this sin behavior. This may take a little more thought, but remember our beliefs always drive our behaviors. Why do you think this is a behavior that you want to engage in? What's the pay-off?

5. For "Consequences" list some of the consequences caused by the behavior. The consequences could be financial, physical, or relational. Try to be specific.

One of the ways we stay stuck in our sin is that we fail to count its costs to us.

6. All sin is ultimately caused by self-deception and false-worship. "God's View" is meant to show you from God's word his perspective on the sin.

7. A spare, blank worksheet is included in case you need extra space to write (see QR Code below). Make as many copies of this as needed.

8. As we have discussed in previous chapters, Satan loves to accuse us and he will seek to use this exercise as a means of heaping shame on us. Keep your thoughts focused on meditating on the truths of Romans 8:31-39. Your identity is not in your sin. Your identity is in Christ. You are his and nothing can ever take you from him. Thoughtfully pray over this passage as you are doing this exercise.

COMFORT IDOLS   DRUG, ALCOHOL ABUSE

SURFACE SINS Drunkenness, Impaired driving, and Taking drugs without an Rx or in excess of Rx

YOUR BEHAVIOR _____
_____
_____

DRIVING BELIEFS _____
_____

_____

CONSEQUENCES _____

_____

_____

GOD'S VIEWS   Mood altering with chemicals creates addiction; God wants us to alter our mood by instead being filled with his Spirit (Eph. 5:18).

COMFORT IDOLS   OVEREATING

SURFACE SINS   Eating too much when stressed, bored, depressed, etc.

YOUR BEHAVIOR _____

_____

_____

DRIVING BELIEFS _____

_____

_____

CONSEQUENCES _____

_____

_____

GOD'S VIEWS   Gluttony is no less an addiction than alcoholism; it will create the same poverty of mind and spirit (Prov. 23:20-21).

COMFORT IDOLS   PORN, LUST

SURFACE SINS   Online porn, magazines, etc., strip clubs, prostitutes, sexual fantasies, objectifying others, and romanticism

YOUR BEHAVIOR _____

_____

_____

DRIVING BELIEFS _____

_____

_____

CONSEQUENCES _____

_____

_____

GOD'S VIEWS The greatest deception of the enemy is that porn and other lusts of the mind and eyes are not as "bad" as physical adultery; there is no difference in God's eyes (Matt. 5:28).

COMFORT IDOLS MATERIALISM, LOVE OF MONEY

SURFACE SINS Living beyonds means, impulsive shopping, hoarding, and greed

YOUR BEHAVIOR _____

_____

_____

DRIVING BELIEFS _____

_____

_____

CONSEQUENCES _____

_____

_____

GOD'S VIEWS Money and materialism have the greatest ability to lead us astray from the faith because they create a sense of independence from God (1 Tim. 6:10).

COMFORT IDOLS SLOTH, LAZINESS

SURFACE SINS Habitual procrastination, treating physical comfort as primary motive for life, and binging on tv and/or internet

YOUR BEHAVIOR _____

_____

DRIVING BELIEFS _____
_____
_____
_____

CONSEQUENCES _____
_____
_____

GOD'S VIEWS   As image bearers of God we are called to act, serve, bless and build in his name and for his glory. We cannot be lazy to the glory of God (1 Cor. 10:31).

COMFORT IDOLS   OBSESSION ABOUT HEALTH

SURFACE SINS   Fear of growing older, obsessing about health, and anxiety about symptoms

YOUR BEHAVIOR _____
_____
_____

DRIVING BELIEFS _____
_____
_____

CONSEQUENCES _____
_____
_____

GOD'S VIEWS   Our fears about our future, including our health, show that we fear God's sovereignty in action in our lives. Even illness and suffering can be meant for good when God is sovereign (Matt 6:25-27).

COMFORT IDOLS   FANTASY

SURFACE SINS   Day-dreaming to avoid facing reality or fantasizing about the future instead of living in the present

YOUR BEHAVIOR   _____
_____
_____

DRIVING BELIEFS   _____
_____
_____

CONSEQUENCES   _____
_____
_____

GOD'S VIEWS   Living in a fantasy world ultimately blinds us to the work God is doing right now. God wants us to meditate on him, the ultimate truth. Our fantasies lie to us (Phil. 4:8).

CONTROL IDOLS   ANGER

SURFACE SINS   Controlling others with anger, defensiveness, raging/
yelling, pouting, punishing, keeping score, and
passive aggressiveness

YOUR BEHAVIOR   _____
_____
_____

DRIVING BELIEFS   _____
_____
_____

CONSEQUENCES   _____
_____
_____

GOD'S VIEWS   Anger towards others shows that we have become
forgetful that God's righteous anger toward us has
passed over us onto Christ (Eph. 4:29-31).

CONTROL IDOLS   FEAR/ANXIETY

SURFACE SINS   "What if" thinking, obsession with bad news / what's
going wrong in the world, fear of future, pessimistic,
and lack of peace

YOUR BEHAVIOR   _____
_____
_____

DRIVING BELIEFS   _____
_____
_____

CONSEQUENCES   _____
_____
_____

GOD'S VIEWS   Fear and anxiety robs us of the moments when we can experience genuine communion with God even in difficult circumstances (Phil. 4:6).

CONTROL IDOLS   OBSESSIVE THINKING

SURFACE SINS   Intrusive thoughts, ritualistic behavior, looping thoughts, and worst case scenario thinking

YOUR BEHAVIOR _____
_____
_____

DRIVING BELIEFS _____
_____
_____

CONSEQUENCES _____
_____
_____

GOD'S VIEWS   Our thoughts will either capture and enslave us or we can capture them for Christ to change (2 Cor. 10:5).

CONTROL IDOLS   RESTRICTING FOOD; BINGING/PURGING

SURFACE SINS   Starving yourself, excessive dieting, overeating so you purge, and over-exercise

YOUR BEHAVIOR _____
_____
_____

DRIVING BELIEFS _____
_____
_____

CONSEQUENCES _____
_____
_____

GOD'S VIEWS Eating disorders are our attempts to control life when things are out of control. But your body is a holy place because God lives there. He bought you with the blood of Christ (1 Cor. 6:19-20).

CONTROL IDOLS   SARCASM, CRITICAL SPIRIT, OR JUDGMENTAL

SURFACE SINS Belittling jokes, scrutinizing others' mistakes, sarcastic jokes, and picking apart words of others

YOUR BEHAVIOR _____
_____
_____

DRIVING BELIEFS _____
_____
_____

CONSEQUENCES _____
_____
_____

GOD'S VIEWS Judging others is the ultimate act of pride in that it presumes to have the knowledge that God has; critical speech says that we love ourselves more than our neighbor (Jas. 4:11-12).

CONTROL IDOLS   SELF HARM

SURFACE SINS Cutting or punching self

YOUR BEHAVIOR _____
_____
_____

DRIVING BELIEFS _____
_____
_____

CONSEQUENCES _____
_____
_____

GOD'S VIEWS   Self-harm is the silent scream. But we are defacing the very home of God. Your body matters to God (1 Cor. 6:19-20).

CONTROL IDOLS   ABUSE OF OTHERS

SURFACE SINS   Physical abuse, sexual abuse, and emotional abuse

YOUR BEHAVIOR _____
_____
_____

DRIVING BELIEFS _____
_____
_____

CONSEQUENCES _____
_____
_____

GOD'S VIEWS   Abuse of any kind is hating the abused person, someone who bears the image of God. How can we hate someone and claim to love God? (1 Jn. 4:20).

PEOPLE IDOLS   WORKS RIGHTEOUSNESS

SURFACE SINS   Behavior determines worth an reward-seeking for good behavior

YOUR BEHAVIOR   _____
_____
_____

DRIVING BELIEFS   _____
_____
_____

CONSEQUENCES   _____
_____
_____

GOD'S VIEWS   God wants us weak in the flesh so we can be strong in him. Boasting in ourselves denies the power we can have in Christ (2 Cor.11:30).

PEOPLE IDOLS   RESCUING

SURFACE SINS   Take on others' consequences, loan money unwisely, treated as a doormat, no boundaries, and need to "save" others

YOUR BEHAVIOR   _____
_____
_____

DRIVING BELIEFS   _____
_____
_____

CONSEQUENCES   _____
_____
_____

GOD'S VIEWS   God's law of sowing and reaping is meant as a loving discipline to help us hate sin. Rescuing keeps people trapped in their sin, which is the ultimate cruelty (Gal. 6:7-8).

PEOPLE IDOLS   APPROVAL SEEKING

SURFACE SINS   Fear of disappointing others, over-extended, make everything about you, need constant reassurance, seeking compliments or affirmation from others

YOUR BEHAVIOR _____
_____
_____

DRIVING BELIEFS _____
_____
_____

CONSEQUENCES _____
_____
_____

GOD'S VIEWS   We stand already approved by God because we are approved in Christ. If we pursue the approval of man then we are really serving ourselves (Gal. 1:10).

PEOPLE IDOLS   EMOTIONAL, PHYSICAL AFFAIR

SURFACE SINS   Poor boundaries with opposite sex, seeking emotional support that spouse alone should provide, and physical adultery

YOUR BEHAVIOR _____
_____
_____

DRIVING BELIEFS _____
_____
_____

CONSEQUENCES _____
_____
_____

GOD'S VIEWS Adultery and emotional unfaithfulness destroy our
intimacy with God and with others (Prov. 6:32).

PEOPLE IDOLS   RELATIONSHIP ADDICTION

SURFACE SINS Look to friends and family members for your sense of
well being, enmeshed relationships (letting others
define your identity), spiral down when relationship
is not well, and over-involvement with your kids'
lives, sports

YOUR BEHAVIOR _____
_____
_____

DRIVING BELIEFS _____
_____
_____

CONSEQUENCES _____
_____
_____

GOD'S VIEWS Rather than looking to people, even people we love
and care about, we must first look to our savior. Only
he can tell us who we really are. Only his love for us is
steadfast (Heb. 12:1-2).

Shame
Complete After Lesson 6

Referring back to your answers in Lesson 6, summarize your struggles with shame (guilt, feeling exposed, feeling like you do not belong or there is something wrong with you):

How does your struggle with shame drive you sin behaviors?

Repentance
Complete as You Work on Lesson 7, 8, and 9

This is a place to capture specific sinful beliefs/thoughts and behaviors you are repenting of. Remember, to repent is to think differently about your sin, by turning away from it and to turn toward God in worship. Repentance is a gift of God's grace, not a work of man, so any moment of repentance should also be joined with a moment of worship for what God has done for you.

Specific false/incomplete beliefs about God and the gospel I am repenting of:

Surface and Heart Idols I am repenting of:

Shameful thought patterns I am repenting of:

Patterns of unforgiveness I am repenting of:

Patterns of mistreating others I am repenting of:

Some specific ways my love/worship for God is growing that fuels my repentance:

Forgiving Others
Complete After Lesson 10

Make a list of people who have harmed you through their sin who you need to forgive.

Who You Need to Forgive	Who You Need to Forgive Them

Set aside time and prayerfully extend forgiveness to all of the individuals listed above. If you cannot extend forgiveness to a person at this time, continue to pray about that until you can. Dialogue with a pastor or Biblical counselor about why you are struggling with unforgiveness. Remember: forgiving someone does not deny that you were hurt in some way. Forgiveness simply surrenders that person to God.

Asking for Forgiveness

Now, make a list of people you have harmed through your sin for which you need to take responsibility and be reconciled. Refer back to the worksheets in Lesson 5 to help you remember whom you have sinned against.

People You Have Harmed	How You Harmed Them

Begin to meet with each person listed above to ask for his or her forgiveness. Refer back to the material in Lesson 10 for suggestions as to how to have a reconciling conversation with that person. Where restitution is needed, make it in that meeting or be prepared to communicate how you will be making restitution.

Your Rhythms of Grace
Complete After Lesson 11

Some who write about spiritual disciplines will often talk about a "rule for life." When they use the term "rule" they are not referring to a rule like a law. Instead they are using the word to mean a template or pattern (which is what a ruler is.) While we have said repeatedly throughout this study that our practice of spiritual disciplines does not change us (only God can do that), practicing them does still benefit us. And unless we have a plan for how and when we will practice the disciplines, we will not be consistent (and miss out on their benefit). That's why we need to have our own personal template or "rule" for practicing the disciplines.

Take some time and write down your plan for practicing some key spiritual disciplines:

1. How many days of the week and what time of the day do you plan to read and meditate on God's word? Where will you do that so that you minimize interruptions and distractions?

2. Setting aside prayers at meals and with your family, when do you plan to have focused prayer time with God?

3. Identify times each week you can practice self-examination to confess sins to God.

4. Who are the people you are in covenant community with and to whom you can share struggles and especially confess your sins? How often do you plan to spend time with them?

ACKNOWLEDGEMENTS

All that I shared in this study bears witness to the power of 2 Tim. 2:2. Nothing here is original but is simply me passing on what has been generously shared with me by many others in the faith. Special thanks are extended to David Bruns, Bruce Henry, and Jimmy Thoma who helped review the study and test it out in small groups, along with countless elders, teammates and friends at Fellowship in Little Rock.

Last, but never least, special thanks go to my wife Leigh, my partner in ministry and constant encourager. All of you remind me time and time again of the hope that I have in Christ alone, my very righteousness and my sanctification. Soli Deo Gloria!

ABOUT THE AUTHOR

Jim Hudson (MA, JD) serves as a pastor and elder at Fellowship Bible Church in Little Rock, Arkansas. His ministry passion is to help others see the wonderful truth that through the Gospel we have all we need for life and godliness. Jim lives in Little Rock with his wife Leigh. While they have no children of their own, in Christ they have many spiritual children and grandchildren.

OTHER GCD
RESOURCES

Visit GCDiscipleship.com/Books

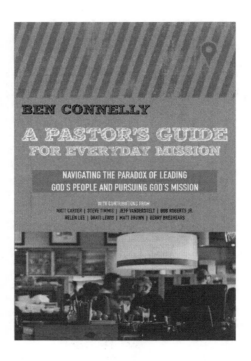

After fifteen plus years of vocational ministry, Ben Connelly had an epiphany. He had missed the great commission. He was really good at keeping Christians happy and really bad at making disciples. *A Pastor's Guide to Everyday Mission* helps those in paid ministry positions rediscover—and live —their life as God's missionaries, even as they minister to God's people.

Missional communities are sending agencies into our neighborhoods, cities, and nations. To be clear, it is not that communities grow in numbers and need to split, or that communities have a pyramid growth chart. Multiplication is a function of a gospel work and empowerment of the Spirit. Leaders and communities are sent out of existing gospel communities because the gospel is advancing and sending us into maturity.

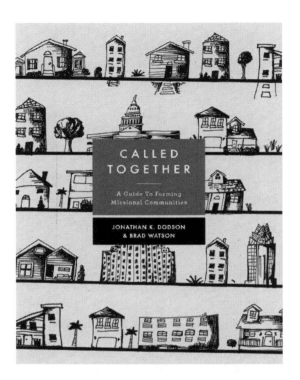

This eight week guide helps communities discover their calling to be and make disciples together. The eight weeks covers important discussions on the gospel, community, and mission while also giving communities next steps to practice what they've talked about.

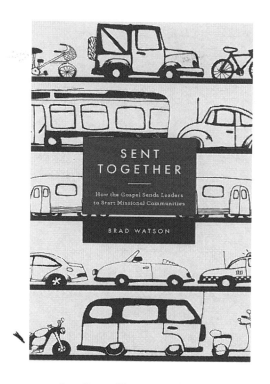

Jesus does not simply call us to be a lovely community together, but he sends us out to our neighborhoods, towns, and cities to declare and demonstrate the gospel. In fact, the gospel beckons men and women to take up the call of leading and starting communities that are sent like Jesus.

Small Town Mission is a practical guide for gospel-centered mission in small towns. If you haven't noticed, people who live in small towns have limited options for restaurants, shopping, and books about mission. Small towns desperately need normal, everyday people like farmers, factory workers, teachers, secretaries, and small business owners who think and act like missionaries to reach their friends, neighbors, co-workers, and extended families for Christ.

THE STORIES WE LIVE

Discovering the True and Better Way of Jesus.

SEAN POST

Foreword by RICK MCKINLEY

"The Bible as a whole is a story, a grand narrative, that grips our hearts, our minds, our imaginations. We join with Jesus and His community on a quest which demands our best effort in the team's mission. The end is glorious indeed. *The Stories We Live* is a great introduction to that grand narrative and also some of the broken stories which distract many. Read, be gripped by the story, and join the quest!"

Gerry Breshears, Professor of Theology, Western Seminary, Portland, OR

Make, Mature, Multiply aims to help you become a disciple who truly understands the full joy of following Jesus. With a wide range of chapters from some of today's most battle-tested disciple-makers, this book is designed for any Christian seeking to know more about being a fully-formed disciple of Jesus who makes, matures, and multiplies fully-formed disciples of Jesus.

everPresent

HOW THE GOSPEL RELOCATES US IN THE PRESENT

By Jeremy Writebol

Foreword by Jonathan Dodson

"*everPresent* does something that most books don't achieve. Most focus either on who God is or what we should do. Jeremy starts with who God is to walk the reader down the path of what God has done, who we are because of God, then points us to understand what we do because of this. I highly recommend picking up *everPresent* to better understand the why and how of the life of those that follow Jesus."

Seth McBee, Executive Team Member, GCM Collective

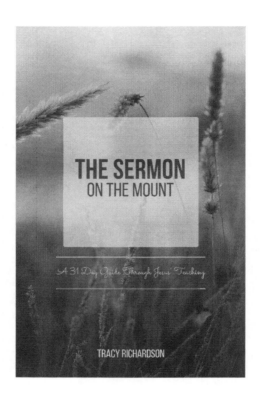

In *The Sermon on the Mount: A 31 Day Guide Through Jesus' Teaching,* Tracy Richardson walks us through Jesus' teaching in hopes that the Spirit will transform the hearts of his disciples. This guide is designed specifically for DNA groups, two to three people, who meet weekly under the leadership of the Spirit.